THOMAS SUMMERS & CO.

THOMAS SUMMERS & CO.

BOATBUILDERS OF FRASERBURGH

MIKE SMYLIE

Front cover: Amethyst steaming in Loch Aline, Sound of Mull, 2019.
(Photo courtesy of Ian MacLean)
Back cover: Summer's shipyard on the Breakwater *c.* 1955.

First published 2020

The History Press
97 St George's Place, Cheltenham,
Gloucestershire, GL 50 3QB
www.thehistorypress.co.uk

British Library Cataloguing in Publication Data.
A catalogue record for this book is available from the British Library.

ISBN 978 0 7509 9219 0

Typesetting and origination by The History Press
Printed in Turkey by Imak

CONTENTS

ACKNOWLEDGEMENTS

I SAID FROM THE VERY beginning of initial discussions about this book in late 2018 that I was only the messenger and that others were responsible for its foundation. Now, although I've written some twenty-five books over the years, I've never literally worked through the medium of social media. However, as a first, this one has evolved from a Facebook page first set up by Shetland mussel fisherman Lindsay Laurenson in 2016 called 'The Wooden Boats of Tommy Summers' with the intention of collecting information about the boats built at this, one of three main yards in Fraserburgh's harbour in the mid-twentieth century. Subsequently, work in this field fell into the hands (fingers?) of two men, both fishermen, Alexander West and Malcolm Burge, who then drove the project forward with gusto and therefore it's wholly due to them that this book has survived the planning process, from cyberspace on to the physical, tangible paper form that books are. I thank them for giving me the chance to learn, as I write, about what is an incredible feat: to produce so many fine craft in such a short period of time.

Yet I feel I must add some words from my co-founder of the 40+ Fishing Boat Association, Mike Craine, who reminded me that it was the Association which started the hunt for Summers boats back in 1999 when, in *Fishing Boats* no. 15, we drew up a list of eighty-five boats from the yard. In time information and photographs of those boats have continued to surface on the Facebook page almost right up to publication. Mike has also added several photographs, as well as background information on some boats.

Others I must thank who have helped along the way, especially in my travels around the coasts of Scotland and sourcing photographs, are: the family of Tommy Summers – Jim Summers, Thomas (Duncan) Summers, Elizabeth and Kenny MacLemman; and then, in no particular order, Charlie Duncan, William

Whyte, Johny Wilson, Sander West, Rob Walker, Jim Mckerracher, Mark Stockl, Stewart Buchan, Grace and Ian Strachan, John Scott, Peter Campbell, Stephen Worthington, Luke Powell and Kenneth Ritchie.

Most of the photographs here have come from the Facebook page where it has been widely publicised that they will be used in this book. I apologise unreservedly if any have been used where the originator was known and not credited. In the event of any omission please contact me care of the publishers so we can rectify for future editions of this book. I am eternally grateful for the contributions from many people of these photos and the ensuing information about the boats in them, as well as, in some cases, helping identify the places in the photos.

A word on photograph quality. In the majority of cases we have had to rely upon photographs that were taken up to seventy years ago by fishermen who are long gone, and these photos have been passed down through many hands and have been often scanned on old scanners, thus the quality has not been the best. I apologise for this as it has been almost impossible to obtain and copy the originals, but I believe it is better to use a poorer-quality photo rather than have no photographic record of a particular vessel when there is no choice amongst the photos available for that vessel.

All of this would have been impossible without the substantial input from Linda Fitzpatrick and the staff at the Scottish Fisheries Museum at Anstruther past and present for the initial work in formulating the various build lists of the four Fraserburgh and Sandhaven boatbuilding yards. We are so lucky to have the SFM and, a year after his passing, I would also like to mention my friend and mentor Dr Robert Prescott whose input to the museum was colossal.

Last but nowhere least, there's my family back home whilst I'm away touring Scotland or simply at home with my head in the clouds as I write. Thanks to them!

Usually I dedicate my books to my children. This time, though, this one is for Tommy, George and Bill, in their memories. Also for Mike Craine who tragically died during the production of this book.

INTRODUCTION

THE FISHING INDUSTRY AT THE end of the Second World War
was quick on the recovery after six years of restricted fishing. Although the
building of Admiralty motor fishing vessels (MFVs) had progressed during the
war, giving work to the Scottish east-coast boatbuilders, as well as serving naval
requirements during the hostilities, it was proposed that the design would be
deemed suitable for the fishing industry afterwards. To this end, those that survived the war were sold off once they were no longer needed by the Admiralty,
and at the same time the demand for new boats increased. Boatyards thrived
because, not only did these MFVs need refitting for fishing but various government acts allowed grants and loans to be made to skippers so that the older
stock of steam drifters and those left from the sailing era could be replaced with
the new breed of dual-purpose motor boats.

In Fraserburgh the three yards of James Noble, J. & G. Forbes of Sandhaven
and William Noble had all been producing these standard MFVs during the
war, and afterwards were busy, so it wasn't surprising locally when a new yard,
opened by three local men, appeared. Tommy Summers & Co., as it was named,
was incredible for the very shortness of its life. In the space of thirteen years,
between 1949 and 1962, the yard produced eighty-nine fishing vessels, which
is no mean feat. Compared with the output of other similar yards, this was far
in excess of their yearly average.

This, then, is the story of those relatively few years, told through records
and personal memories. Mostly it's a litany of the series of excellent and hardy
fishing boats, which have been grouped into three separate categories. Many
of these craft survive today, especially the smaller ones, which in itself serves as
a testament to their superb design and solid construction.

If I were asked to describe the work of Tommy Summers in a word, the
nearest I can think of is 'innovational', or possibly even 'revolutionary',
for his work in the design of fishing boats was just that. Moreover he was

hard-working, inspirational and dedicated, although later on in life it appears he regarded himself as a failure. Nothing can be further from the truth and, in my mind, I've learnt through the process of writing that the sense of his achievement is simply overwhelming. But this book is about the boatbuilding yard and all those others that worked in it, and it must be remembered that he was one part – if a major one indeed – of that team. Unfortunately it has been pretty impossible to learn much about his partners George McLeman and Bill Duthie, although a couple of informants were able to pass on character assessments which glowed as bright as the Northern Lights! Three partners then, of somewhat equal integrity, together formed a firm that, because it was so short-lived, can be regarded as a sort of time capsule of boatbuilding in the mid-twentieth century.

Fraserburgh harbour from an old postcard with yawls in the foreground and the boatbuilding shed of James Noble and the harbour slipway used by Thomas Summers to launch yawls.

1

A LITTLE BIT OF HISTORY

FRASERBURGH – ORIGINALLY AN AMALGAMATION of the harbour of Faithlie, first built about 1547, on the eastern side of the north-west tip of Aberdeenshire and the fishing village of Broadsea (originally Seatown) to the north-west around the bay – was laid out as a new town in the sixteenth century by the local landowning Fraser family of Philorth (hence Fraser's burgh or 'Frazersburgh' as one mapmaker put it in 1747) a time after it had become a Royal Burgh in 1601. Built to compete with Peterhead and Aberdeen, it was initially the herring fishing, and subsequently the white fishery, that created the harbour (and town) as it is now. But it was Broadsea that was originally

Broadsea beach prior to a harbour being built for beach-based fishing craft.

the home of the fishermen and, in 1789, it had forty-two fishermen working off the beach with small open boats, twenty-nine of whom had the surname Noble. There were seven boats each crewed by six men and it has been said that they sailed as far as Barra Head, on the west coast, in their search for fish.

Faithlie was little more than a couple of quays surrounding a sandy beach where boats could be drawn up and, prior to the nineteenth century, was the domain of the soldiers and trading boats. Presumably it was exposed to the south-east. By the early nineteenth century the North Pier had been extended and the South Harbour added. This was a time when the herring fishing was rapidly expanding after government interaction in the 1790s. Fraserburgh then became an important herring station during the early summer season and, presumably, the Broadsea men based themselves there.

By 1815 bounties for the herring fishing had been introduced for small craft and the east coast of Scotland's herring fishing turned from being a cottage industry to a commercial fishery. That year, as John Cranna tells us in *Fraserburgh, Past and Present*:

> The boats had no decks whatever, and measured about 20 feet of keel and 12 feet of beam. The crews depended as much upon the oars as the sails for going to and coming from the fishing grounds. The craft never went more than a few miles from the shore in quest of the herring. This accounts for the comparatively small loss of life at sea in these early years. Caught in a gale thirty or forty miles at sea, these cockle shells would have instantly foundered, with results which need not be conjured up. The crews, however, excellent judges of the weather, kept the harbour when lowering clouds appeared, and if at sea, smelt danger from afar, and promptly sought the friendly shelter of port before the fury of the tempest overtook them. Thus were they able nearly a hundred years ago to prosecute their calling in comparative safety, frail though their boats were.

This tends to contradict their sailing to the west coast, yet further developments in the nineteenth century created a much larger harbour as the herring fishing flourished and boats sailed further afield. The number of boats participating in the herring fishing in the district increased rapidly so that by 1830 there were 214 Fraserburgh boats, twenty-four from Peterhead and thirty-four from Rosehearty. This suggests that there were only local boats working out of the harbour though Cranna reports that boats from the Firth of Forth and a few from the north came. At the same time there were thirty fish-curing yards dotted around the town, as Cranna says:

… in the most out-of-the-way places. Messrs. Bruce, for instance, cured on a little bit of ground facing Broad Street and Shore Street, immediately to the south of the Crown Hotel. Curing plots were being freely let off at the entrance to the Links, about or near where the railway station now is, and several firms cured there. The trade was slowly but surely consolidating at Fraserburgh. In the year 1830 the catch of herrings in the Fraserburgh district, which included Peterhead, etc., touched the very respectable figures of 56,182 crans, while the number of curers for Fraserburgh alone was 30, being two more than in 1828.

Boat design altered after the great south-easterly storm in August 1848 when many fishing boats were lost along the east coast, with tragic fatalities amongst the fishers. Many of these were overcome by the sheer force of the waves when returning in the face of the storm to unsafe harbours, but seemingly the Fraserburgh men survived intact whereas in Peterhead there were thirty-one casualties with twenty-eight boats wrecked. But the storm forced Parliament to act and the subsequent report submitted by Captain John Washington made various recommendations with regard to harbour improvement and vessel design, as well as the phasing out of the error of plying fishermen with whisky in part payment for their labours! However, Fraserburgh did have its own storm to remember in 1850 when a north-westerly gale forced boats onto the sands. In the face of tradegy only one life was lost, with ten boats driven ashore.

In the harbour the Balaclava Pier was added over the Inch Rocks in the 1850s to create more protection and later the South Pier was built, followed by the Balaclava Harbour works. Boats also became larger due to improved build-ing techniques in carvel construction where planks are laid side by side instead of overlapping or clinker (clench) building. Decks were added to the previously undecked craft, affording greater seaworthiness and safety at sea.

As more and more men were enticed into fishing – what else was there? – the demand for fishing boats grew, as did that for trading vessels to carry the herring off to markets. With the arrival of the railway to Fraserburgh in 1865, allowing fish to be carried away to the centres of population such as Edinburgh and Glasgow, the landings increased rapidly. Some maritime industries suffered – sailmaking and rope works in the main – as these commodities could be produced elsewhere cheaper, and consequently Fraserburgh saw no incoming industrialisation on a large scale.

Fishing became the main occupation of the second half of the nineteenth century, at first aboard the great Zulus and fifies, with their powerful lug rigs, and then with the introduction of steam drifters and trawlers. In the 1880s

Small open yawls upon the bach at Inverallochy at the end of the nineteenth century.

Fraserburgh harbour simply filled with fishing boats prior to 1939.

there were some sixty curers working in the town. On one night in July 1884, 667 boats landed 20,010 cran of herring, and the herring lassies were kept busy processing this catch into barrels. But such was the enormity of the catch, and the fact that the fish were small, that even though they worked all night, the women were unable to gut it all, and with more being landed the next day, some 4,000 cran were dumped in the harbour with plenty more being carted to farmers who laid it on their fields as fertiliser.

Fish processing (an improvement from 'curing') was an important part of the industry and supplied the British army with rations in the Boer War and again in both the First and Second World Wars. In the early 1920s, with the advent of the internal combustion engine, so began the last great development in wooden fishing-boat design with cruiser-sterned herring drifters, canoe-sterned ring-netters and double-ended seiners leading to, later, transom-sterned craft as motor power increased. Further harbour expansion brought about the Faithlie Basin, the completion of which ended the expansion of the harbour, although improvements continued and do so right up to this day.

Needless to say, boats needed boatbuilders and Fraserburgh has had some well-known names in that respect over time. One of the first documented was a Mr John Dalrymple, a member of a family that came to Fraserburgh from the Firth of Forth, who had a facility at Black Sands in the early nineteenth century.

Another was John Webster, described as a shipbuilder who employed fifty carpenters and who commenced work in 1840 but had ceased by 1887. It appears he was originally from Aberdeen but chose Fraserburgh to set up his yard. Mr Weatherhead – a name well known further south – worked for some twenty-five years up to 1900, while another name was Scott & Yule from 1890–1915. Both Mr Scott and Mr Yule had been apprentices to Webster and took over his dilapidated yard. This company was, according to Cranna in 1914, 'kept very busy building fishing boats known as steam drifters, which in some measure, fills up the gap caused by the collapse of shipbuilding.' However, within a year the yard had closed, a reflection maybe on the general state of shipbuilding. Alexander Noble, an apprentice from Scott & Yule's, opened a yard adjacent to Provost Anderson's Jetty in 1898 but handed over to his son Wilson Noble in 1910, a name that survived until 1959. Unfortunately there seem to be no records of the boats that yard built prior to 1911, but that year it is known he built two Zulu-type boats: *Violet*, FR451 and *Vesper*. *Violet* still survives in the US. By the 1920s they were building seiners although they had also built motor minesweepers during the war.

During the first half of the twentieth century, boatbuilding, along with the fishing industry itself, saw its ups and downs caused by a mixture of depression,

In the 1920s many boats changed over to the seine net, a Danish invention. Huge coils of rope were needed for this mode of fishing and here Fraserburgh men were kept fully employed tarring the ropes used by the fishermen by dragging them through a tank of tar.

recession and war. Wilson's younger brother James, one of Wilson's apprentices, decided yacht building would be more beneficial than relying on fishing boats and so he left his brother and started his own yard in 1932 at the north end of the harbour. However, new yachts never came his way but fishing boat orders did, and stuck! So much so that he was later joined by another brother, Charles. From building their first boat *Wistaria*, BCK116, that year, to their final vessel in 1981, they completed 223 vessels including twenty Admiralty MFVs during the war.

At the same time, a little to the west of Fraserburgh, the Forbes family was producing fine craft of repute, something it had been building at the head of the small harbour of Sandhaven since 1884. Another company, Buchan, Hall & Mitchell started up in 1922 (partners: Peter Buchan, Hugh Hall and William Mitchell) which has been documented as building fishing vessels at their premises at the southern end of the Faithlie Basin.

Finally, in 1948, three carpenters from James Noble's yard – all apprenticed there – decided to set up their own business and it was agreed by these men that the company would be called Thomas Summers & Co.

2

TOMMY SUMMERS & CO.

THESE THREE WERE LOCAL MEN: Thomas Summers, always known as Tommy, George McLeman and Bill Duthie, all of whom were equal partners having put up their own money as stakes to start the business. It had not been a sudden decision as, working at James Noble's yard, they had seen signs of the beginnings of a building boom. Over several months they'd made their preparations. Tommy was to be the head designer, George was to take charge of building the yawls, as that was where they saw their immediate future, and Bill was to supervise the cutting of all the major timbers that make up a wooden boat: the centreline structure, frames, strengthening and planking. They'd even made up moulds for a yawl in readiness!

A word of explanation here. The word 'yawl' is a variation of 'yole', often used to describe small fishing boats on the east coast of Scotland and in the northern isles: hence Stroma yole, Orkney yole and the Shetland variant Ness yoal. The word comes from the Scandinavian *yol* meaning small boat, usually double-ended, originally with one mast. Hereabout it was generally considered to be a small fifie-type vessel (double-ended and with upright stem and sterns) much in favour amongst the fishermen of Fraserburgh where they are often referred to as Fraserburgh yoles. But the yawls here are regarded as being the much larger vessels – the predecessors, if you want – and in this book they will always be referred to as 'yawls' in deference to those who consider it such because, for one thing, this was what was painted in large letters upon the western face of the Saltoun Jetty, near to its junction with the South Pier, where they tended to congregate in Fraserburgh's harbour in their latter days. I apologise to those others who have, for whatever reason, regarded them as Fraserburgh 'yoles', and can only repeat that some consider the 'yoles' as being the forerunners of the yawls in that they were smaller in size. Many referred to these small boats as fifie yawls and Zulu skiffs, depending on what part of the coast they were from. Terminology can sometimes be very frustrating after the event when, at the time of their use, they were referred to simply as 'yawl' or even 'boat' in the spoken word form and never written down. As I have said, we will call them yawls, or 'Broch yawls' as they were known to many, and even 'Ripper yawls', the reason for which will become clear.

Small fishing vessels were nothing new in Fraserburgh as we've seen, and both of Noble's yards and that of Forbes at Sandhaven had built them since before the war. Initially smaller, they evolved to being generally around the 32–35ft mark in overall length and were considered easy to handle for inshore lining and creel fishing by one or two crew. By the time the Summers yard opened for business in 1949, the sail had been abandoned and all were fitted with 30–40hp engines, depending on size.

T. Summers & Co. leased and operated from a site on Steamboat Quay, along the Balaclava Pier before it becomes the Balaclava (or North) Breakwater, a place pretty exposed to the North Sea. Facilities were sparse as there was no electricity on site, simply a small shed for storage of tools and the engine-driven bandsaw with another even smaller shed acting as office and store. Over time they were able to erect more small buildings, whilst possibly a quarter of the yard space was taken over by the storage of timber whilst it seasoned for a year or more before being cut up and used.

Boats were built stern facing the town across the Balaclava Outer Harbour. Today, somewhat ironically, the site houses the stores and offices for the local family-owned fishing companies of the Westward Fishing Co., the Klondyke Fishing Co. and the Buchan family-owned Lunar Fishing, whose fishing dynasty started off on a boat built on this site in 1954, the 70ft *Lunar Bow*, PD425.

The first boat Summers built was the 34ft (10.3m) yawl *Fisher Boys*, FR54. She was launched in 1949 and was immediately recognisable as being different in that she had a cruiser stern, for it is believed that Tommy Summers, showing his innovative skills, was the first designer to incorporate a cruiser stern into the Fraserburgh fleet of small yawls, mirroring the development of the larger herring boats from a decade or more before. This yawl was on order by local Broch businessman George Duthie (no relation to Bill) who owned the Northern Engineering Company and who also had a fleet of vessels that he leased out to local skippers. Although he'd had new boats built, he favoured the yawls and had even bought older ones from fishermen which he had re-engined to be leased out. This was at a time when motor power was something new and demand was such that there was a waiting list for his reconditioned yawls. In 1946 he commissioned Forbes to build three larger dual-purpose motor boats – *Golden Dawn*, FR317, *Boy George*, FR135 and *Bobby Stephen*, FR157.

Top to bottom: The yard with two big boats under construction and between them the slipway for launching; Another view of the yard with men working on three vessels; Caulking up a boat in September 1957: teams of men would caulk down a seam each, walking backwards in time; Summers' staff including John Skene Sim, Bobby Ritchie and George Summers.

When Duthie decided he wanted a new yawl a couple of years later, he heard about the plans for a new firm and thus it wasn't surprising when he chose them to commission a new yawl. This was partly due to word coming out that Tommy Summers had incorporated a cruiser stern into his new yawl design, something that Duthie found both intriguing and somewhat attractively practical. He also realised that the added weight of engine into the hull meant that added buoyancy aft was fast becoming vital as engine power, thus weight, increased. Prior to this, the general consensus was that to bend the timber planking around the shape of the cruiser stern was almost impossible on such a small vessel and easier with a more linear curvature that the pointed stern offered. But the new yard was bucking the trend and, with improvements in boat construction and steam techniques, bending the planking round in such a shape was found to be possible. Cruiser-sterned yawls were, for the first time, a reality and *Fisher Boys* presumably appeared impressive.

Although it's not known whether or not the firm employed apprentices and other skilled workers from the outset, it is presumed that they soon did take on staff as another order for a yawl soon followed, hard on the heels of *Fisher Boys* taking to the water. This, the 31ft (9.5m) *Daisy*, FR78, was ordered by J. Stephens of Cairnbulg. Both these initial yawls were fitted with 33hp Kelvin J3 diesel engines. Because there was no slipway from Steamboat Quay, these yawls had to be manhandled along the Balaclava Pier with the boats lying over on their side upon wooden rollers and being pulled using a lorry as well as manpower and, in some cases, a steam roller. The boats were then launched into the harbour using the harbour slipway in front of James Noble's yard.

George Duthie, happy with the results from his first yawl, then ordered another in 1950, this being *Just Reward*, FR117, similar in size to *Fisher Boys*, again with a K3 engine. Unlike *Daisy*, she had a small dodger, or shelter, aft for the helmsman, the forerunner to fitting wheelhouses on later boats. Unfortunately, this was the last new boat he commissioned before being lost at sea when the lifeboat *Charles and John Kennedy* foundered in the 1953 disaster. He had been an engineer aboard the vessel. The lifeboat had gone to escort some small fishing boats – probably yawls – to safety and was returning back to harbour when she was hit by a huge wave and capsized, with only one crew member surviving.

But before work had begun on *Just Reward*, the first of Summers' bigger boats, the 70ft (21.5m) *Ocean Gleaner*, BF600, had been ordered by Alex Watt of Gardenstown who presumably had been satisfied with the general accord to the quality of Summers' work. Now, with two boats under construction, the workforce must have increased in size. Though this vessel was almost twice the size of the yawls, there was plenty of room in the yard to build vessels side by side. On the other hand, when it came to launching, it was a different kettle of fish. There was no way that a 70-footer could be hauled along the quayside to the slipway so a different method had to be worked out. What eventually was decided upon by Tommy was somewhat dramatic and involved dropping the boat off the end of the quay into the harbour at high water when there was only an 8ft drop! So successful was this method of launching that subsequent vessels followed. Some mean feat it must have been and it seems that any sub-sequent launch attracted a crowd with many folk running 'doon Kirk Brae' to see such an event. Indeed, in the nineteenth century, when the yards were turn-ing out ships, Cranna mentions that 'thousands' turned out to watch launches though possibly fishing boats didn't quite draw the same attention!

Tommy Summers started by building a wooden frame beneath the boat which enabled it to be moved on launch day without damaging the timber of the keel. Stout ropes were attached to the boat and carried across the harbour to two lor-ries which, on the signal, pulled the boat over into the water whilst ropes from the stern controlled the forward motion. Thus the boat splashed into the harbour and there are some fantastic photos from the 1950s of this process.

By the end of 1952 Thomas Summers & Co. had built four more of these bigger boats of a similar size: *Star of Buchan*, FR309, *Gleaner*, FR291, *Morning Star*, PD234 and *Radiant Way*, FR329. *Morning Star* was almost 76ft (23.1m) in length. These boats were fitted with either Kelvin or Gardner engines. In 1953, the local newspaper *Weekly Journal* ran an article about these launches after witnessing that of *Fisher Queen*, FR331, in January 1953, writing that, 'There is sure to be a large crowd, for no one would miss this thrilling spectacle. To the layman, the boat has all the appearance of plunging to the bottom of the har-bour, and there is always a gasp from the crowd as it hits the water.'

Looking at the various photos of the launching process, it's easy to under-stand the gasp from onlookers. One respondent remembers her dad, who worked in the yard, telling her how he was once strapped aboard a boat during one particular launch. The 8ft lunge would certainly shake anyone to the bones!

But in one instance, during the launch of *Lilacina*, BF395, the communica-tions broke down, which could have ended in a disastrous situation. In true pre-health-and-safety days, the way to notify the driver of the lorry across the harbour was to wave a white handkerchief when he was to start the pull that would drag the boat into the harbour. On this occasion, with ten minutes to go until high water, Tommy and his guests had 'gone for a cup of tea' whilst waiting. But Jimmy, the man with the handkerchief, had seen his lady friend across the harbour and, forgetting for a moment his duty, waved with his white hanky at her to come over. Sadly, the lorry driver mistook this for the signal and, starting up his engine, engaged reverse and tensioned the tow rope before commencing the drag. *Lilacina* was then prematurely sent into the water whilst those on the quay were dashing along to grab the ropes to prevent her from crashing into the dock the other side. Luckily the launch was successful and no damage occurred, but this served as a warning for future launches and modification of the white hanky signal was deemed necessary.

A steady stream of orders came in for the firm which meant a series of boats were constructed and launched with success. The firm was growing in stature and recommendation. In 1955, when building of the larger 80ft liner *Northern Venture*, FR14 – his largest to date – was underway, he decided this boat couldn't be dropped off the quay. The answer was to build a concrete slipway by cutting into the quayside by several feet and thus reducing the height between quay and water. After an initial success with *Northern Venture*, this method was then used to launch all the ensuing bigger boats, although the yawls continued to be dragged along to the slip by Noble's yard. However, even with the cutout in the quay, the outline of which can be seen today, this simply reduced the height of the drop. There was still a distance of 3ft or so to drop down.

Whilst Tommy was supervising the building and launching of the big boats, Bill chopping up an ever-increasing amount of larch and oak timber and George McLeman busy overseeing the build of the yawls, they also developed their forty-footer range, which had begun in 1951 with the launch of three of these: *Gladiolus*, BF255, *Silver Fern*, BF369 and *Ha'burn*, BF268. Again these were engined with Kelvins or Gardners. The majority of these so-called 'forty-footers' measured just under 40ft, *Silver Fern* being the exception. Being under 40ft, they were able to use the seine net within the 3-mile limit.

It didn't take long for the boats produced by the yard to gain favour amongst local skippers. Considering the basic conditions of the yard and its position exposed to the elements of the North Sea, they really did build some of the finest vessels. Many fine words have been spoken about the lines of the boats that Tommy Summers designed. They say he had the eye for a kindly vessel and they also state with conviction that he could tell the seakeeping qualities of any vessel by simply considering her lines. He, for sure, had a faithful following and this didn't seem to diminish as his career went on. Today, whilst the number of boats, and fishermen, has declined, there's the same conviction that these boats were amongst the best.

Operating a busy yard on the Steamboat Quay, a place open to the elements, is something that today is hard to fully understand. But, being exposed to whatever the sea could throw at a yard sitting upon an open quayside, it thrived. Even for the workforce to reach their place of work in the morning was sometimes a dash along the pier avoiding the worst of the waves in stormy conditions by taking shelter every so often. Work was hard and only slightly eased when electricity reached the yard in 1953 when the beacon at the end of the pier was electrified. Prior to that, whereas other yards had electric hand tools, they had to work manually. Just boring out the hole for the shaft aperture in the sternpost could take two men several days using a hand boring tool.

Today, amongst the few fishermen and many more ex-fishermen, the firm Tommy Summers & Co. is renowned more for its yawls than its bigger boats. That's not to say the largest vessels, along with the forty-footers, weren't in demand, but for inshore fishing these yawls became widespread in their use. Often there were several in varying states of construction upon the quay at any one time. It's also worth mentioning that the yard also built some pleasure boats. One yacht was called *Duncan Fletcher*, whilst there's a motor cruiser called *Creole* that was built in 1962 and which is today based in Lochinver. Also Thomas (Duncan) Summers mentioned some cabin cruisers and that his father took at least one to the boat show in Earls Court at some time.

The harbour slip in front of the James Noble yard where today the dry dock is. The yawl in the foreground is *The Lily*, FR182, 35ft LOA, built by Forbes in 1950.

Here the *Grateful*, FR270, is being prepared for moving for her launch.

The *Grateful* now in front of the James Noble yard – a new-built inside in view –
prior to launching.

The other point about the company was that, although it was generally in existence for a relatively short period – from 1949 to 1962 – it managed to produce some eighty-nine fishing vessels in sizes ranging from *Daisy* at 31ft (9.5m) to both *WFP*, LT310, and *Ada Kirby*, LT72, at 97ft (29.5m). In all, some thirty-one yawls were built on the quay, often by men that were apprentices, as it was generally the case then that learning the ropes on the smaller boats enabled the same men to progress to the larger ones. They were often referred to as 'ripper yawls' amongst the fishermen because many were fishing with ripper handlines for cod predominantly over wrecks after the Second World War as cod stocks declined. Although ripper lining had been practised around Fraserburgh and south of Aberdeen (and in the East Neuk) from the early 1900s using small skiffs and fifie yawls (small fifies in reality up to approximately 30ft), it was only as echo sounders improved fishing capability and motorisation increased possibilities, that the ripper yawls evolved, perfect for the job of setting ripper lines.

Tommy Summers designed all the vessels that they built and launched except for three. When the Grimsby & Brixham Trawler Company Ltd approached the yard to build seven vessels, Tommy thought the order too much for the small yard so he offered to split it with the Forbes yard which was experiencing a lull in orders. The deal that they then agreed was that Forbes would design all the craft and build four whilst Summers would build three Danish-type seiners, and these were the only boats he didn't design throughout the life of the yard. These were, as were the Forbes vessels, all named after birds, with the Summers boats being *Shearbill*, GY571, *Moorhen*, GY593 and *Ferriby*, GY621, all 52ft (15.85m) in length.

It's almost impossible to relate on paper the atmosphere of expectation and excitement at any boatyard immersed in the building of wooden boats. But there's a short cine film of the Summers yard taken in 1955, which gives a wonderful insight into those heady days, when health and safety was largely non-existent, when men in flat caps worked in what was really cutting-edge boatbuilding, resulting in some of the finest fishing boats seen anyway. No yellow hi-viz wear, no safety harnesses, wooden ladders climbed without having undergone a ladder safety course, working at height with hand tools (and later electric ones) but each man knowing exactly what was expected. There's them hauling a frame into place atop the keel, the launching off the quay of two big boats, *Westhaven*, FR375, and *Present Help*, FR53. Then comes the green-painted *Girl May*, PD283, being named by, presumably, the skipper's wife, with a huge crowd around the harbourside. Tommy is there, dressed formally but looking slightly worried as he was overseeing the launch. The boat is then off, just quick enough so that the stern plunges

Morning Star, PD234, being launched off the quayside in 1952.

The dramatic launch of *Fisher Queen*, FR331, off the quayside a year later. Within another year, work to construct a slipway of sorts had begun.

The launch of *Westhaven* in 1954, possibly the first boat launched after the construction of the slipway.

into the water first with an almighty splash, with the momentum carrying the rest of the boat over the precipice so that the stem doesn't scrape its way down the edge of the quay. The crowd cheers (I added that bit as there's only music, but my guess is that they did!) and Tommy once again looks on as the men aboard, balance regained, stand proud under the Union Jacks that fly at both ends. It's all nostalgic stuff now that wooden boatbuilding for the fishing industry is at an end, but at the same time it is an historical testament to the determination of what the company achieved in its short time. It's also a timely reminder that, although the name Tommy Summers figures predominantly, both George McLeman and Bill Duthie were, as were the whole workforce and ancillary workers, just as responsible for the success of the company.

The yawls were generally inshore vessels, normally working within 30 miles of the coast at the line fishing, though there were, as always, exceptions. The bigger boats, 70ft and more, were mostly dual-purpose boats, working the drift net for herring or seining for whitefish, depending on the time of year. But as the herring stocks gradually depleted in the 1950s, some found it hard to profit from seining alone. Others, like *Northern Venture*, were built for the great line fishery away offshore, this one living up to her name 'venturing north' towards Iceland, though it has been said that the Broch fishers weren't generally keen on long-lining! The *Bdellium*, FR185, was the first Broch boat that went to the purse seine in 1967.

As well as building the hulls of wooden boats, there was a need for steel-work and engineering, and Bill Kirkness and Doug Bailey ran an engineering company at the back of the yard, undertaking many of the tasks needed in the construction process. Often much of the engine work was completed after the boat was launched.

The Summers boats were primarily powered with Kelvin or Gardner engines, the former being based in Dobbies Loan, Glasgow, a place well known throughout the fishing communities of the west coast, whilst Gardner engines had their roots in the Barton Hall Engine works at Patricroft, near Manchester. Although somewhat rivals, both were familiar names in all fishing circles because, between the two of them, they engined much of the British fishing fleet in the last century. Looking through the lists of boats it becomes obvious that Kelvin engines were favoured for the smaller yawls, with Gardners for the bigger boats, while the forty-footers accounted for a ratio of 65:35 Gardner to Kelvin. Apart from these two well-known names, there were, according to the lists of Summers boats, four boats launched with Bolinder motors installed, one with a Blackstone and three smaller-powered Listers, although the two com-panies had merged by this time (ironically one of Lister's old factories where they manufactured their pipes is at the bottom of my garden!), two AK Diesels and one Russell Newbery and one Mack. The AK Diesels had horsepowers far exceeding anything else at 300hp, perfect for trawling. In the run of time, as engine technology improved, mirroring the development of fishing methods, boats often had their engines exchanged for higher-powered models to suit their modes of fishing.

In regard to engine construction and development, it's worth noting that both Frederick Russell and William Newbery were apprenticed to Henry Royce, him-self having first set up business as a mechanic in Manchester's Stratford Road, yards away from where Lawrence Gardner first set himself up as a machinist in 1868.

In 1959 the fishing industry once again was in the doldrums with the her-ring industry in serious decline. When, in July of that year, *Wayfarer*, FR190, was launched off Steamboat Quay, watched by hundreds of holidaymakers who gasped at the way the boat plunged off the quay into the harbour in a flurry of spray, according to the report in one of the local newspapers, the same paper suggested this might be the last launch of its type as T. Summers & Co. were to shortly take over the Balaclava yard of Wilson Noble & Co., across the harbour on Bissett's Quay. This yard had been long-standing: Wilson Noble had taken over the business from his father Alex in 1910 and had built a long stream of fishing vessels until the slump at the end of the 1950s, and was now closing down. Yet it wasn't until 1960 that Thomas Summers & Co. actually began building boats at what was, in actuality, a much more comprehensive yard, and the presumption was that all his bigger boats would be constructed there rather than on Steamboat Quay. At that time Tommy was quoted as saying, 'I don't say we'll never do a quayside launch – but if we do, there won't be many. It will depend on whether we need an extra berth.' Obviously the need was there because there were seven more such launches over the next few years and only two vessels, surprisingly, were built at the Wilson Noble yard.

Today there seems no reason for this inconsistency for at the Balaclava yard the workforce had the benefit of an enclosed shed and far greater facilities for building their craft. In fact, it has been said that this yard looked the healthiest out of the three still in business at the time immediately prior to Wilson Noble closing down. For Summers, the 75ft (22.9m) *Bdellium*, FR185, was the first boat launched at this yard, a large dual-purpose seiner-trawler. *Guiding Star*, LH382, followed, whilst work on others continued across at Steamboat Quay.

Then came the shock. Suddenly, in 1962, at a time when it was generally believed the firm was doing so well with two yards in work, news came that Tommy Summers & Co. was to close. Work at Steamboat Quay ceased immediately whilst the last boat built at the Wilson Noble yard was a Kemrock yacht, which was a job passed on from Roderick Forbes. Across at the Steamboat Quay yard, the three yawls *Daybreak*, FR250, *Speedwell*, FR316, and *Boyne Vale*, BF266, had been the final vessels. Thus, with the Summers yards ceasing work, only J. & G. Forbes and James Noble continued the Fraserburgh tradition of wooden boatbuilding into the era of new designs for fishing craft. Buchan, Hall & Mitchell continued in wooden boat repairs, and still do today.

Although the yard of Tommy Summers & Co. only ran for a comparatively short time – 1948 to 1962 – the boats they turned out were of the highest quality and many remain afloat today, some even still fishing. One of the most fascinating facts is obvious when reading through the principal details of each boat. They are, on the whole, all of differing specifications. If you imagined that the thirty-one yawls were of a standard design, you'd be wrong. Are the fourteen 'forty-footers' all 40ft in length? No! Are the forty-three bigger boats built to one general size and shape? No! In other words, each vessel was drawn up and a half model built, resulting in a shape unique to that vessel. The only exceptions were the three boats designed by the Forbes yard for Grimsby owners and the two large great liners *WFP* and *Ada Kirby* destined for Lowestoft owners.

As I've already mentioned, Tommy made the half models of his designs. He also made complete scale models of boats and when Princess Margaret and Lord Snowdon came to open the new Fraserburgh Academy in September 1962, they were presented with a model of a fishing boat that Tommy had made. When the royals found out who had made it, they asked for him to be fetched so they could thank him. The reply came that 'he was doing the dishes' at the time but, as his daughter later remarked, that would have been a first! Nevertheless he was thanked in person.

There's no doubt that Fraserburgh produced some fine fishing craft, as did the whole of the east coast of Scotland. In the 1950s, apart from Summers, Forbes, Wilson Noble and James Noble, many other companies were still active such as Weatherheads of Eyemouth, Millers of St Monans, Smith & Hutton of Anstruther, Gerrards of Arbroath, Richard Irvin of Peterhead, Watt of Gardenstown and Stephens of Banff (these last two later becoming Macduffs), amongst others. Yet only Summers worked wholly in the open, with no building shed, unlike all the others. So to produce so much, with minimal working infrastructure, makes their achievements over such a short period even more spectacular.

Their boats have served fishing communities throughout Britain and some have even sailed across the Atlantic to Canada and back, with at least one, *Star of Buchan*, transferring to New Zealand where she is now the *Fellowship*. Those that remain today are often sought after, such is the respect and even loyalty felt by many for these craft. Out of the eighty-nine built, fifteen still actively fish whilst several others have been converted for pleasure and still sail. However, it would be safe to say the most popular and enduring of T. Summers & Co. boats were the yawls, which ranged from 31 to 37ft in length. Of the thirty-one built, thirteen are still licensed for commercial fishing with another couple of uncertain whereabouts. Surely that speaks for itself.

3

BUILDING WOODEN BOATS

WOODEN BOATBUILDING OF TRADITIONAL COASTAL craft in Britain has, in the main, evolved from two different influences: that of clinker construction from the Scandinavian countries to the east and that of carvel construction from the countries to the south of us.

Clinker craft – constructed with planks that overlap each other and are riveted together with copper nails – are generally built shell-first using transverse moulds fixed to the keel to guide the shape, with the strengthening of the ribs being added once the shell is completed. This method was inherited from the Viking settlers who first came to Britain as invaders in the late eighth century and heavily influenced many aspects of British life. This method was perfectly suited to building small double-ended fishing boats up to about 40ft, and these were commonplace all around the Scottish coast and down into many traditional fishing communities, especially those beach-based ones such as Hastings, Cromer and Filey, to name a few. It is still commonplace in many parts, especially the Northern Isles, Outer Hebrides, Northern Ireland and parts of the east coast of England.

Carvel construction, on the other hand, necessitates the building of a framework first, consisting basically of a keel, stem and sternpost and frames, to which the outer planking is then fixed, with the planks meeting edge-on. The gap between these planks is then filled with caulking matter and sealed. Today's carvel construction has its roots in the Mediterranean where a similar method was used in building a shell-first structure by joining the planks using tenons in the way biscuit jointing is done today. This evolved into what we recognise today as carvel by building a strong framework. In Scotland this gained precedence in the 1860s as larger fishing boats were needed in their ever-seeking quest for fish in distant fishing grounds and this is the way fishing boats were built at T. Summers & Co. So here follows the layman's basic step-by-step guide to wooden boatbuilding, without of course the finesse that the skilled men in any yard would have added from their experience. I apologise for this elementary approach to what is in essence an art form.

Boat building always begins in the drawing office, where lines plans, half models and constructional plans are made. Here Tommy Summers was in charge, this being his domain. The proposed boat will, by this time, have been discussed between him and the owner who will have conveyed his requirements as to size, mode of fishing and cost. Half models are perhaps far more important than is often recognised, and many boatbuilders have mentioned how, by making a half model and eyeing the feel of it, they judge the final shape of the boat. A half model is made by shaping wood to the outline of each waterline, the thickness of each piece of wood being the separation between waterlines on the lines plan. Once these are all glued together, the surplus timber is then removed and the shape faired. Thus the hull can be examined and, if necessary, shaved down if the shape isn't quite right. The lines plan can be adjusted to suit and, if the half model is considered too fine, sometimes it is necessary to make another with fuller lines. However, it is said that Tommy Summers never drew a lines plan and all measurements were either taken from the half model he'd built or indeed straight from his memory.

Once the shape of the vessel has been finalised, probably in discussion between the designer and the skipper, the process moves to lofting where the body of the vessel is drawn out on a large flat floor at full size, called the lofting floor. Tommy Summers' sons still remember him drawing out chalk lines on the lofting floor without any means of measurement, simply chalking the shape of the hull using his eye.

At the same time, although the yard will already have a good stock of sea-soned timber, the pieces needed for this build will have been chosen and some perhaps ordered from suppliers. Summers used the well-known timber importer and merchant Barchards of Hull for some of their timber. Generally, this will have consisted of oak for the framework and larch planking with Oregon pine for the deck. Much of the European larch might well have been sourced from local yards, perhaps within 50 miles of Fraserburgh. Sided for at least a year, all the timber will have dried to an acceptable level of moisture content. Bill Duthie would have been kept busy sorting through the timber, picking out the best slabs and sawing these up to the requisite sizes. Although it's often said that the apprentices constructed the smaller boats in the Summers yard, the same fellows were said to have often used offcuts from the larger boats to build the smaller ones. Given that many of the smaller yawls have survived today whereas the largest ones haven't, this was obviously a successful use of timber resources. Moreover, I must add that the reason the bigger boats haven't survived is partly down to decommissioning whereas the small yawls were never eligible for decommissioning grants.

Construction begins by setting up the keel on blocks of a suitable height. The keel is the main fore-and-aft strength of the boat and is, if possible, made from one hefty piece of oak though often has to be scarphed to join two pieces. The rabbet, a groove either side to receive the garboard plank, has to be chiselled out. Once this is done, the backbone can be set up. To one end of the keel is attached the stem, using a mortise and tenon joint and a knee, fixed using wooden pegs, to add strength. An apron fixes to the back of this to take the ends of the planking. The sternpost is fitted at the other end in a similar manner where the deadwood – consisting of reinforcing pieces of oak built up to replace a stern knee that adds lateral strength to the keel – is fitted, each being bolted on. A curved fashion piece, following the shape of the cruiser stern, is then butted up against the sternpost and supported with a knee atop. Either side, aprons are fitted alongside this fashion piece and sandwiched between the sternpost to add strength, the aprons then taking the plank ends. Once the rudder stock is fitted by drilling through the fashion piece, this will strengthen the cruiser stern as it's supported by the heel of the keel.

The hog, a stout piece of timber wider and not as deep as the keel, is fitted atop the keel, to allow the garboard – or bottom – strake to be attached as an alternative to carving out the rabbet. Thus some boats do not have a hog, though most of Tommy Summers & Co. boats, it appears, did. Others have a keelson which is fixed over the floors, as described above.

Each frame is made up of several pieces: the floor acts as the base of the structure, overlapping the keel with 'wings' either side to which the bottom futtocks attach, with the top futtocks above, forming the symmetrical frame. The futtocks are joined by staggering against the adjoining one, or, if the frames are doubled, another set of futtocks alongside that cross the joint. To extract these differing shapes from the lofting floor, moulds, thin pieces of wood, are made up for each frame, copying their shape. These moulds are then used to trace the same shape onto the slabs of oak, always choosing pieces where the grain follows the shape. The pieces are then cut out and bevelled to suit the longitudinal shape of the boat, and the various components joined together to make up each frame. Once complete, and when the backbone is ready, these are then lifted onto the keel at the marked station points, and, in the case of yawls (and many other working boats), fixed using iron dumps through the floor, hog and into the keel, to stiffen the whole structure. Once the whole vessel is thus framed, a keelson that runs from the stem to sternpost clamps over the top of the floors to lock the structure in place. Temporary supports and shores will ensure the structure stays stable. The frames then have to be faired even though they will have been cut with a bevel across their outer face. Fairing with an adze smooths out any errors in the shape so that before any planking can be added, the whole hull must be so faired.

The beamshelf – sometimes called the inwale – follows the inside of the top of the frames just below deck level and longitudinally clamps up the top of the frames. As its name implies, this also acts as a shelf for the deck beams to fit upon. These will have been cut from suitable pieces of oak to give some camber to the deck to ensure seawater flows away. Stringers also are fixed on the inside of the frames, at the turn of the bilge where the futtocks join, as additional longitudinal strength to the structure.

At the same time, the hull planking will have progressed once the fairing is complete. Wide larch planking – occasionally oak is preferred – is prepared and, starting at the top with the sheer strake, to hold the frames in place (though sometimes two teams work so that the other can start at the garboard plank against the keel) is nailed on. They then meet at the turn of the bilge with the shutter plank. Each strake (which sometimes consists of more than one plank because of the length of the vessel and the available timber) is in turn cut to shape and then offered up to be marked with fixing holes and then steamed as necessary, before being clamped onto the frames and fixed using large iron nails called dumps, although one iron rivet through plank and frame can be veri-fied on the yawls. Planks have to be cut out to take into account that the shape differs along its entire length and their individual shape is determined using spile battens fixed to the frames as a temporary measure. Where the planks are butt-jointed, this occurs on a suitable frame and strakes are always staggered onto different frames. The top strake at deck level each side (the sheer strake) is usually thicker than the normal planking to form a strong ring with the addi-tion of the beamshelf on the inside. This stiffens the whole vessel. Sometimes a stringer strake is added at the turn of the bilge which, too, is slightly thicker and takes a short bilge keel.

Once the planking of the hull is complete and faired, the gaps between the strakes have to be caulked once they have been primed with red lead, although these days red lead substitutes have to be used. To fill the gaps oakum or tarred tow is used. This is rolled over itself as it is pushed into the seam – gauging as it's called – with a caulking iron and mallet. The caulker has a range of caulking irons to use and an expert can tell the tightness of the oakum just by the ring of the caulking iron when hit with his mallet. Get a few people caulking at

Setting up the deadwood in a modern-day boatyard.

Top to bottom: Each frame is made up of separate pieces, this one being a doubled frame; Setting the frames up onto the keel; Work progresses on setting up the frames on one of the last large Scottish wooden fishing boats, late 1990s.

The completed framed body of a Cornish fishing vessel.

the same time and it's like music to the ears! Once the entire seam has so been filled, the caulker moves to the next. Caulking is much more of a job than is often recognised, and I've seen examples of all sorts of weird stuff poked into seams in old boats to try and stop water ingress. However, there's no alternative to proper oakum or similar material which expands once the boat is in the water. Once the whole vessel has been caulked, the seams are then filled with putty and linseed oil, again with the addition of red lead or its modern-day substitute, to fair them off.

The integrity of the hull should now be complete, and attention will turn to the deck. Deck beams have already been installed whilst, to form the positions of intended hatches, longitudinal carlins have to be fitted between deck beams with half beams filling between the carlin and side of the boat. Oak knees are used to strengthen the joint between hull and deck, and the deck itself.

The upper frame heads (the extensions of the frames above deck) form the bulwarks each side whilst the covering boards fit over the beam shelves and sheer strakes either side with cutouts where the upper frame heads stand through. The covering board should be as long as possible, with the grain following the curve of the deck. The deck itself can then be laid which is then caulked and the seams sealed with hot tar. Generally Oregon pine, imported from Canada, was used for the deck for it is straight-grained, strong and hard-wearing under fishermen's boots and their heavy gear. The propeller shaft and rudder will have been installed by now. Engine bearers, in larch to reduce vibration, are fitted across frames to suit its position.

Often the boat is launched at this time, once the hull is painted or varnished, depending on finish. Once afloat, work can be resumed by way of the hatches. Machinery such as the engine, generator, bilge pumps, fuel and water tanks and other gear is installed before the wheelhouse, which has been built outside of the boat and hoisted aboard and securely fixed down. In the case of the yawls, this was dropped into a lowered portion of the deck, thus keeping the windage of the boat to a minimum. The bulwarks are built up at the same time, whilst below decks bulkheads can be fitted with accommodation built in. Generally this was in the forward end in the case of the yawls and forty-footers but in the after end of the bigger boats. Also below decks the pounds are built in the fish room and net store, winches and other fishing gear installed, with elec-trics, navigation equipment and internal furnishings. Final ballasting of the boat canthen take place to ensure she floats at the designed waterline. Sea trials test all aspects of the vessel and its machinery and general performance to ensure the finished vessel lives up to, or even exceeds, expectations before its ultimate handover to the client is completed.

Normally, each boat would take a couple of months to build and often more than one was under construction at any one time. The one contract we've seen states a '3 month' construction period. Considering Thomas Summers & Co. built some eighty-nine fishing vessels in a little over thirteen years, that's an incredible average of almost seven vessels each year. Compare that to James Noble who built 223 boats in forty-nine years (average four and a half per year). In one year, 1955, eleven vessels were built. One verbal report stated that, in one case, a boat was built in four weeks, though the informant was unsure as to the size. Even if it was a yawl, it's almost unbelievable. However, given that they were regarded as both attractive and favoured by the Fraserburgh, St Combs, Inverallochy and Cairnbulg skippers, and that many have survived into the twenty-first century, it proves their resilience and good build quality. They might have been built in the open, using age-old methods, but they were surely amongst the very best boats built anywhere in the world.

Planking underway in the case of the last Scottish fishing vessel.

Planking at the keel of the boat, showing the way the planks are let into keel and sternpost.

Planking underway where a butt joint has to be made.

Inside view of the frames of a wooden vessel, 2010.

Planking complete!

A deck view showing how the stanchions are fitted to the top of the frames, with a double beamshelf bolted on. The bulwark planking fits to the outside of the stanchions whilst the deck beam will sit atop the beamshelf.

However you look at traditional wooden boatbuilding, there's not much room for today's brand of mechanisation in its processes as there are in other walks of life. You can use technology to cut out the shape of frames and even pre-bevel them, but the completed basic structure would still need fairing because timber is a live material and it moves without any encouragement. The strakes still need to be steamed and attached by hand, nails bashed in, caulking done in the age-old way, copper riveted over in unison. There's room for cutting timber by machine but it has to be manually attached. There's no excuse and this is, perhaps, why wooden boatbuilding isn't practised much these days in modern Britain, although there are still some practitioners who persevere with success.

But wood is both aesthetic and workable, even if it is expensive today. Back in the 1950s, when labour was easily available and oak and larch in easy supply, wooden fishing boats thrived. Thus it's no wonder that Scottish-built fishing boats have been held in such high esteem the world over since those heady days following the Second World War. They were, indeed, sea-kindly, seaworthy, substantial, successful and, to many because of their shape, even sexy!

4

SOME BOATS AND
THEIR SOGGY ENDINGS

BOATS BY THEIR VERY NATURE generally live in water, their intended purpose in life to work in extreme situations. Thus it's hardly surprising that many become wrecked through a number of causes in what can be an intemperate and hostile environment. However, when they sink it's always a sad occurrence even when life is not lost. When lives are lost, it becomes a devastating tragedy, the tentacles of which stretch far and wide amongst seafaring communities, something that Britain's small, close-knit coastal fishing communities have had to live with over the centuries. Although the Summers boats are widely regarded as being hardy and durable, some suffered the indignity of being lost at sea and one such disaster befell three yawls in one particular catastrophe in 1959.

THE OCTOBER 1959 GALE

One of these boats was *Ocean Swell*, FR69. Built in 1958 for G. Masson of Sandhaven, she was little over a year old when fishing the grounds off Rattray Head one beautiful calm October day when there was hardly a breath of wind. It was so calm that fishing was an opportunity not to be missed even though a gale was forecast for later. Crew member Billy Clark, also from Sandhaven, was drinking tea in the fo'c'sle when, without any warning at all, a storm broke, much earlier than forecast, with winds from the north-north-east. Not for the first time off the east coast of Scotland did winds from this direction arrive unannounced. Billy recounted his story at the time.

The shock of abrupt change to the weather made him drop his mug. Peering out he realised a maelstrom had pounced, the sea a boiling fury, often lost in the flurries of snow being thrown at them. He raced for the bilge pump seeing seawater gushing over the deck, whilst the skipper battled to keep the boat heading into the seas, fearing any attempt to turn and run for home. The Gardner 42hp continued throbbing away as crew and boat fought against the elements, the boat rising up huge waves in wind said to be over 100mph.

All day they battled, he said afterwards, and at times he prayed, thinking they were done for. Just how long could the small boat survive the onslaught she was receiving. But then, all of a sudden, the Fraserburgh lifeboat *Duchess of Kent*, a replacement after the loss of the Watson-class lifeboat *John and Charles Kennedy* in 1953, appeared through the grey haze of a blizzard on their starboard side. They'd not sent flares up but those ashore knew there was trouble and somehow the lifeboat crew found them in the harshest of conditions. The lifeboat stood by waiting, and another fishing boat appeared out of the gloom. Eventually it was possible to turn about and the lifeboat began to escort both boats back to Peterhead as Fraserburgh harbour was impossible to enter in these conditions. But a gigantic wave, 'roaring down like thunder' hit *Ocean Swell* broadside and suddenly the wheelhouse was full of water as the boat righted itself after capsizing. With the engine still running, the boat swamped, the lights flicking on and off and boxes floating in the flooded fo'c'sle, the lifeboat came in. Fisherman Alex John Duthie was coxswain that day as the coxswain and second coxswain were both out fishing, and he had a scratch crew aboard. Nevertheless, the skill with which he managed to bring the lifeboat alongside the stricken vessel, his propellors thrashing away in the water as he controlled the lifeboat, was incredible, and Billy recalls how he then manhandled the unconscious skipper out to waiting hands to haul him aboard before he himself was helped aboard by crewman John Stephen.

The lifeboat and the other fishing vessel made port and the crew were taken ashore. But the story didn't end there. Later that afternoon, as dark was coming, the 230-ton Grimsby trawler *Yesso*, GY610, was on her way north to the Faroese fishing grounds. Skipper George Loades of Cleethorpes saw the floating vessel and called Stonehaven radio to report this. He was informed that the vessel had been abandoned that afternoon and thus he hove-to and awaited a decrease in the wind before getting a tow aboard at 11 o'clock the following day. At 4 o'clock that afternoon Fraserburgh boatman Peter Strachan chugged out in the pilot boat to tow the vessel into the inner harbour at Peterhead. Amazingly, the wheelhouse was still intact. Thus she was salvaged and renamed *Girl Avril*. Tommy Summers was called down to Peterhead to inspect the boat and there's a photo of him with skippers Masson and Loades aboard the craft.

The Grimsby trawler *Yesso*, GY610, which towed the *Ocean Swell* back into Peterhead.

The crew of the *Morning Star*, FR286. The remains of the boat can still be seen where she was wrecked on Kilundine Point in the Sound of Mull.

The *Easter Morn*, FR372, after she was beached.

Equally amazing in the photo is the intact lights that also survived a capsizing. Indeed, the quality of fittings must have been top-notch.

John Stephen was coxswain of the same lifeboat when, in 1970, she went to the aid of the Danish fishing vessel *Opal*. The lifeboat capsized, with five of her six-man crew perishing. John Stephen was one of these, as was mechanic Fred Kirkness, who had been aboard when *Ocean Swell* capsized.

Although there was no loss of life aboard the *Ocean Swell*, which has allowed us to learn of the hideous conditions, other yawls suffered from this gale, termed 'Tuesday's killer gale' by the local newspapers in which lives were taken away. *Morning Star*, FR47, also built in 1958, was lost with her two crew William Strachan (49) from Cairnbulg and Andrew Duthie (62) from Inverallochy. The boat was never recovered and thus we know no more about what befell these men and their vessel.

At the same time, Andrew Duthie (50) from Inverallochy was drowned when *Easter Morn*, FR372, was forced ashore and wrecked. However, she was later recovered, repaired and renamed *Boy Alec*.

In October 1970 the Grimsby seiner *Ferriby*, GY621, one of the three designed by Forbes and built by T. Summers & Co., was fishing the North Sea when she had to dodge gales and leave her fishing gear in the water. The last contact by radio had been on the Wednesday and when, in an area 120 miles east of the river Tyne, a liferaft was picked up the following Friday, a search was immediately begun. Boats and a helicopter joined but the fate of the boat was decided when part of the wheelhouse and other wreckage were discovered. There were four members of the crew including the skipper, and no survivors were ever found. We can only assume that she was swamped in the full force of the savage wind and seas.

OTHER LOSSES

Edna, renamed *Accord*, and registered as UL20, was once owned by entrepreneur and baronet Sir Patrick Grant of Dalvey. He has been described as a one-time gamekeeper and west-coast fisherman and, it appears, he bought *Accord* to fish for prawns off the west coast. At some point she was damaged whilst tied up alongside a pier. She was then towed, presumably, into sheltered waters to have the damage repaired but she began to take in water, and sank somewhere in the waters of Kylesku, on the north-west coast of Scotland.

In 1982 *Girl Betty* caught fire whilst fishing and sank without loss of life. She was working out of Thurso at the time. On the other hand, *Winsome*, FR45, sank at her mooring off Ardwell without any apparent reason.

Ha'burn had a couple of interesting episodes in her life. Not long after her launch in 1951 she was transferred to Aberdeen and was often kept in the river Dee. In 1978, a cold winter, the river iced over and damaged the hull to such a state that she sank. She was later raised and taken to Nairn for repair and subsequently worked prawn trawls from Lossiemouth and Burghead from where, incidentally, the forty-footer *Illustrious* was working until 2018. *Ha'burn* then crossed the country and went to the Clyde, registered as BA170. Whilst trawling she caught a mine in the net and the bomb disposal folk were informed and soon appeared. They clambered aboard and inspected the mine which was hanging in the net. They set a fuse but this was obviously slightly too short so that, by the time the net was let go, the bomb went off too close to the vessel and damaged the hull. Taking on water, the boat was taken back to Largs and, after inspection, found to be irreparable and eventually cut up in the marina there.

The 1952-built *Morning Star*, PD234, skippered by her co-owner George Duncan, was the 1955 Prunier Trophy winner. Her catch of just short of 211 cran was landed at Great Yarmouth on 1 November that year. At auction she made £946 and the fish were taken on grounds 35 miles north-east of Great Yarmouth.

In April 1973 *Morning Star* re-registered as FR286, went ashore and was wrecked in the Sound of Mull whilst being towed by *Golden Quest* from Tobermory to Oban for repairs. It appears that she was spending the night in Tobermory and when the engine wouldn't start early the next morning, they decided a tow was the best option. When cutting the corner on the northern side of the loch in the dark, both boats grounded on the rocks at Kilundine Point, Morvern, in the early hours of Monday, 16 April. The *Golden Quest* managed to free herself and take on the six crew of the *Morning Star* which didn't.

The story then goes that Tobermory diver Richard Greaves, with the boat's timbers still visible at low water, salvaged the Gardner engine and lifted it into a rubber dinghy and carried it over to the Salen Pier where, using an old Claymore derrick, he hauled it ashore and it lay for several years.

In 1962 *Scottish Maid*, BF50, was another boat that ran aground very close to Cape Wrath on a very dark, windy night. John Scott's father was the skipper and John recounted his story: 'On that night,' he told me, 'there was a south-west gale blowing with driving rain. She went onto the rocks, named on the Admiralty chart as "Duslic Rock" whilst steaming east.' The rock itself lies a bit over a mile off the Cape itself, to the north-east. John continued:

> Because there was a strong tide running west, the boat came off but was badly damaged. While the crew manned the hand pumps my father steered the boat towards the wee inlet. He knew there was an inlet somewhere in that area but not exactly where it was. It was dark with heavy rain, and no radar in those days, but he managed to find where the inlet was. She sank at the jetty. When daylight came men from the east coast came to patch the hull but the wind changed direction to north-east, the swell got up and that finished the salvage operation and she broke up. Some said it was sheer luck they found that inlet, but my father reckoned God was with them to guide.

Parts of the Gardner engine and the keel are still visible after sixty years, lying close to the small jetty which, too, is marked on the chart.

In 1973 *Fisher Queen*, FR331, ran aground on the north-west coast of the small island of Gunna in the Gunna Sound between Coll and Tiree, and sank before being wrecked by the force of the wind and tide.

In 1966 *Radiant Way*, FR239, was wrecked off Stoer Point in the north-west of Scotland.

In 1960 *Gleaner*, FR291, was wrecked off Shetland.

In 1991, *Girl Helen*, by this time renamed *Avalon 2*, TH243, was in collision in fog with a tanker in the English Channel. She managed to get to shallow water where she sank and was subsequently blown up.

Northern Venture, FR14, was the dream boat of three brothers, James, Andrew and George Summers and their shipmate James Duthie, all from Cairnbulg. Launched in 1955, she was a new breed of motor great-liner, built to withstand the heavy waters of the North Atlantic in search of halibut and was, at the time, the largest vessel in the Fraserburgh fleet. After almost forty years of service, including many years trawling after giving up lining in the 1960s, she sank off Shetland in calm seas, due to taking on water. The whole sinking was filmed from aboard the lifeboat that took on all the crew before she went down. A sad end indeed to a great boat.

Margaret Rose, as *Prospective*, BF400, sank in the middle of the Minch in 1989, east of Barra, and is marked on the chart. It appears she started taking on water although the sea was smooth, and a nearby boat managed to get all the crew off before she sank.

DECOMMISSIONING

Decommissioning was a European policy to reduce fishing capability by paying fishermen to take their boats out of the industry, for which they would be paid. The system was administered by the national government of each individual nation. Stupidly this resulted in hundreds of perfectly seaworthy boats being chopped up as governments were unable to differentiate between the private use of these boats subsequent to decommissioning and those fishing. Thus some historically important vessels were scrapped whilst three survived the ordeal in Britain. Summers boats were not exempt from being destroyed in this way:

> *Star Divine* – decommissioned and scrapped at Inverness in 1993.
> *Wayfarer* – decommissioned and cut up to make sheds at Newlyn in 2008.

This instance reminds us of the small Zulu *Muirneag* from Stornoway that was ultimately chopped up and turned into fencing posts in the 1950s – such an undignified end for a superb vessel. Moreover *Wayfarer* was the last big Summers boat to be de-registered and thus the end of an era.

5

AFTER THE YARD

IF IT SHOCKED THE GENERAL fishing community of Fraserburgh that T. Summers & Co. closed down without much warning, it must have been much more of a shock to the three directors who had achieved so much in such a short time. It probably sent shockwaves down the paths of the other boatbuilders although, as mentioned, they survived to fight another day. James Noble continued until 1976, but that's another Fraserburgh story, and Forbes longer.

What is known is that all three partners in the business came away without the benefit of any wealth. Any money they invested in the project had disappeared and no doubt there will have been a certain amount of accusation at the time. It has been said on numerous occasions that all of the partners were excellent craftsmen yet not the best at the business aspect of running a company, and that might have contributed to their financial woes. The early boats, it has been suggested, might have been sold for a bit less than their real value although, for a new business, that's not unusual. Getting fishermen to keep up payments on their boats was probably something the company had to deal with as seldom would full payment be taken on the handover of the vessel. Some would have received government funding as, for example, was the case with *Janet*, FR166, the owner of which, George Traves, received a mortgage of £2,601 from the White Fish Authority (see Appendix C), whilst others will have been supplied to fishermen 'on tick'.

Tommy Summers got a job with Timbacraft, a company in Shandon, on the west coast, building wooden craft. The owner of the company was a fellow named Peter Boyle and a few years earlier, in 1959 and 1960, Tommy had taken his family for holidays at Rhu, staying in a house belonging to this Peter Boyle. Thus Boyle offered him the job, which he accepted. It was while he was working there that he took lodgings at Garelochhead and, through the owner of the lodgings, met Jock and Peter McKickan. Peter was a boatbuilder although the family had been fishing for generations. They'd wanted to build a new boat and quickly persuaded Tommy to design them one. This he did – the half model still exists, the only Summers one that does – and they bought timber from up at Arrochar which was sawn up and slabbed and floated down the loch to Portincaple where the boat was built. Tommy oversaw the setting up of the frames and then the deck was fitted as they were working out in the open. They then planked the starboard side before Tommy left and he only saw the boat afterwards when she was finished. Thus the 12.16m *Jeannie Stella*, RO50, was launched in 1964 with a Kelvin 66hp K3 engine and is still fishing to this day after a recent refurbishment, based in Port Seton and registered TT277.

Peter's nephew, Peter Campbell, today lives on the site where she was built, along with other members of the family. Sadly Peter McKichan died in November 2018, a time when this book was only at a planning stage. Peter told me how he remembered his uncle saying how hard grafting Tommy Summers was. He recalls them saying that the original half model was of a previous 44-footer and they cut the model down to just under 40ft to suit the Clyde restrictions on fishing boats. He also mentioned that all the gear used to build the boat still exists today on the site – the steamer and bandsaw for instance. They fished the boat until his uncle Peter grew too old to work and sold her to Tarbert where, although fishing, she became a bit run down, and then was sold to the east coast where she's been recently refurbished.

Tommy then worked periods back in Fraserburgh on the *Briar*, FR48, which had been built by Wilson Noble in 1934. For three or four years he worked at Buchan, Hall & Mitchells and then was again back on the west coast, aboard the trawler *Constellation*. It appears the west coast was close to his heart and he tried to persuade his family to move over there when he was offered the managerial job at a yard at Kyle of Lochalsh. His wife refused to move, having elderly parents in Fraserburgh to look after. Another time he was offered a job in South Africa which was refused on the same grounds.

He was a keen footballer in his younger days as an apprentice with James Noble until an adze caused a huge rip down the back of his right leg and finished off any chance of playing again. He later became Chairman of the Fraserburgh Football Club and, with all three partners being keen on the club, the company often sponsored it. Today he's remembered as being somewhat shy and suffering from having that feeling of failure, although his achievement in the yard was outstanding. I got the impression talking to his family that, although he sincerely wanted to be a family man happy at home with his wife and three children, there was something of an adventurer inside him which might have drawn him away from them, something I understand all too well.

The launch of *Jeannie Stella*, RO50, at Portincaple, Long Loch in 1964.
(Courtesy Peter Campbell)

After a drink his wicked sense of humour was said to emerge! But, like so many, he smoked Senior Service fags like a chimney, and eventually succumbed to lung cancer and died in 1993, at the age of 69.

The closing of the yard seemed to physically affect George McLeman the most. Although he worked briefly at Buchan, Hall & Mitchells, within a year his health had taken a serious dive and in 1963 he died. He is remembered by many as a fine Christian man who was also a superb cabinet maker. Several of his church pews still survive in unexpected corners, one being with his daughter Grace and another in one of Fraserburgh's many net stores.

Bill Duthie was described to me as the 'most honest and Godly man', yet he is difficult to trace. It is known that he went to work at the J. & G. Forbes yard in Sandhaven, but otherwise no further details are known at present. That yard closed in 1990 although they did keep their small repair yard in Fraserburgh, close to the James Noble yard, open for several years after that. I'm told Bill's son is still around the area though we failed to make contact with him.

I asked Tommy Summers' three children – now in their 60s and 70s – about their most enduring memories of the yard. Elizabeth, the youngest, was only 6 when it closed but she remembered the smell of timber and tar. It seems the kids were never allowed down the quay when water was breaking over the top, and even today there's a notice saying cars cannot drive down with breaking waves. But there was something else: the excitement of a launch, when all the family was there, dressed to the nines, along with the new owner and his family, and the throngs lining the quay to watch. Something they mentioned, as did Grace Strachan, George McLeman's daughter, was the lemonade and cake they had whenever there was a launch. For small kids in the 1950s that was as big a splash as that of the boat slipping over the quay into the harbour.

6

A FEW TWENTY-FIRST-CENTURY SURVIVORS

LAST YEAR I WAS BACK in Port Penrhyn, Bangor, to catch up with my boatbuilding mate Scott Metcalfe who was busy on his second Danish fishing boat conversion, *Klevia*, whilst working juggling other bread-and-butter jobs he had to keep his business alive. As we wandered around looking at the boats in the yard he pointed out one that was in the process of being lifted onto a low loader on the other side of the dock: 'That's Jim McKerracher's Tommy Summers boat he's sold on. He's just bought another that's in the yard over there. *Morning Star* I think though he's not sure.'

That was my first direct contact with a Summers boat as I glanced across the covered yard behind Scott's sheds, and walked over. The first direct contact, I mean, as, although I must have seen some during visits to Fraserburgh and Peterhead over the years, it was the first time I had peered into the inside, given Jim had removed various planks. But this boat wasn't the original *Morning Star* of course, as we now know, but the one launched as *Speedwell* in 1962. Jim said:

> She was in Gosport when I found her, in the mud. I crawled over her and she seemed okay but when we got her back here, she was worse than I'd thought. Rotten deck beams, carlins, parts of the hull, some awful repairs. I guess I was a bit disappointed as the scantlings are a bit skipped in places. Maybe it's something to do with the geographical area she's worked in over her life, but she's not as beefy as others I've had. She seems fine below the waterline but above is going to need a lot of work, deck, deck beams, knees, the lot. She's a bit flatter in the bottom than others I've had too. I heard that she was over-hauled by a bloke called Hector Handyside some years ago.

Hector was the renowned coble builder from Seahouses in Northumberland and I wouldn't have thought he'd have skimped on work.

Anyway, this was why the one on the low loader, *Sceptre*, he'd passed on to somebody to complete the restoration, as having two at once was, he believed, a step too far. Nevertheless Jim knows his Summers yawls as this will be the sixth he's worked upon. He started with *Just Reward* in the 1990s, a boat he subsequently fished before selling her, and which was lost off Ireland. Then there was *Ocean Swell* which is now fishing from Blyth, renamed *Venture*, BH179; and then came *Daybreak* that he had bought in the Isle of Man before selling her on. She was unfortunately wrecked with a broken back only recently, during the gale that devastated the marina in Holyhead in 2018. By then, he had started on *Sceptre* which had been renamed *Graceful Morn*, and which he sold on to work on *Morning Star*, ex-*Speedwell*. There was also the forty-footer *Summer Rose* that he'd had to almost rebuild before he bought *Sceptre*, and which remains out of the water in Port Penrhyn still under conversion to a liveaboard. Furthermore, he has worked on another small yawl, this one being converted back to fishing after being rigged as a yacht. However, she was a James Millers of St Monans-built vessel so doesn't count against the Summers boats, although it can be argued that this enabled him to draw added experience from working on different constructions.

I asked Jim what makes a Summers yawl so worth restoring. 'The size speaks for itself,' he replied. 'A dream boat for young men who wouldn't be able to work something much larger. And their general shape and style. Tommy Summers made a name for himself in certain quarters and those Fraserburgh boats were perfect.'

Like Jim and many others, Alexander West has a fatal attraction to these vessels. As one of Fraserburgh's youngest skippers (he was Young Skipper of the Year in 2016), he skippers the family's modern trawler *Virtuous*, FR253, the name of which has been handed down through several generations. Not surprisingly, this gave him the impetus to start looking into the history of these craft.

The first *Virtuous*, FR353, was a Summers yawl, built in 1953 for his great grandfather Alex West and brother Jimmy. Jimmy being the older was skipper whilst Alex named the boat. Another brother Georgie worked with their father (also Jimmy) aboard the Forbes-built *Goodway*, FR216. Together brothers Jimmy and Alex worked *Virtuous* for four years before, in 1957, selling her to Peterhead where she kept the same name and took on the registration PD49 in place of FR353. She fished for a number of years before being converted for pleasure around 2006 and today sits outside a house in Skarfskerry, Caithness.

Clockwise from above: *Gracious* on the pontoon at Fraserburgh, along with *Fertile*, FR 152. (Courtesy Alexander West); *Virtuous*, FR 353, heading out of Balaclava Basin, Fraserburgh. At the helm is James (Jimmy) West and his younger brother Alex West standing for'ard of dodge, the shelter over the helmsman. (Courtesy Alexander West); Aboard *Gracious*: Alex West and his son Sander, aged 8 or 9. (Courtesy Alexander West); *Gracious* sorting and unloading the catch at Killibegs. (Courtesy Ph. M. Smith)

Sander West leaning on the derrick aboard, as *Gracious* heads out of Fraserburgh, fish boxes ready to be filled and deflated buoy and deck wash hose over the side. (Courtesy Alexander West)

It was at the time that *Virtuous* was sold that Alex commissioned Thomas Summers & Co. to build *Gracious*, FR167, and, not long afterwards, Jimmy purchased another Summers yawl, *Shamariah*, FR245, when it was only a couple of years old. Alex's son Sander West joined his uncle Jimmy as crew after leaving school at the end of 1963, and recalls during his time on board that they spent periods at Inverness fishing for sprats, pairing with *Harvest Lily*. Four years later Sander joined his father on *Gracious*, his father remaining with him until retirement in 1967.

The boat remained in the family until 1998, during which time Sander recalls time spent every year at the fishing, rippering with her in summer, jigging for mackerel and setting sma-lines in the winter. At that time she was sold to Gilbert Buchan of Killibegs on the west coast of Ireland and she was later converted for pleasure. However, her fishing career didn't finish then and she was later re-registered and today continues fishing from Rosroe Pier, Killary, County Galway.

Sander explained his methods of fishing to me in great detail. The sma-lines he set consisted of 1,200 hooks although one line only had 600 hooks and was called a 'halfie'. Each crew member had two halfies and there were three crew aboard *Gracious*. Each line was baited with mussels prior to sailing, with Sander recounting how he remembered his grandmother splitting the mussels. Mussels for lines were generally obtained from places such as Tain, Newburgh,

Findhorn and even Wales. A few yawls sailed over to Tain and beached, and the mussels were scooped up into the boats, which returned with a full load. Lines were set around slack water, all joined together in one long train, and hauled before the tide strengthened.

Rippering, for which the yawls were well suited, consisted of a hand line to which was attached a specially curved solid cylinder of lead with a short thin metal wire protruding from the bottom. A nylon line was tied through a loop and three or four short snoods off this nylon line led to hooks with lures made from selected dyed feathers or rubber, though in more recent years florists' ribbon was adapted. At the end of the line was another lighter lump of lead which had either a series of four hooks or one single hook. Thus the weighted ripper line was heaved overboard and set just above the seabed in, over the best grounds, some 25 fathoms about 7 miles offshore on a flat, firm seabed, and jerked continuously up and down for cod. Each crew had his own ripper, with one man at the bow, one aft and the other amidships. To prevent any tangling due to the wind blowing the boat, the yawls, with their small-powered engines, could be left slight astern to stem the drift of the wind, the rudder left hard over to port. Once cod stocks declined in the North Sea due to trawling, they tended to set their ripper lines over wrecks which, given the number of wartime wrecks

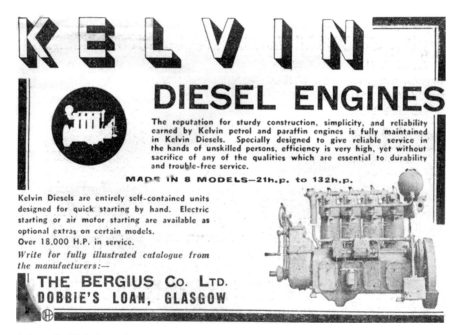
Advert for Kelvin engines.

Advert for Gardner engines.

off the waters around Fraserburgh, gave them lots of choice. The trawlers couldn't reach these grounds! To prevent wear over the gunwale where the line would otherwise constantly rub, a special ripper stick, made from oak, slotted perfectly over the gunwale, over which the lines ran. I saw Sander's stick, now residing in Alexander's garage, with its many years of wear etched into grooves.

More family connections with Summers boats came from his grandmother's side with the two boats of the Ritchie family of Inverallochy: *Green Pastures*, FR 37, in 1954 and *Quiet Waters*, FR 253, in 1960. That port letter and number (PLN) has now passed over to the present *Virtuous*, a boat which was replaced with a new build from Whitby in late 2019.

There's an unusual coincidence about the launch of *Green Pastures*. Under a heading 'Twins join the Fishing Fleet' in the local paper, it notes that two seine-net boats were launched in the north-east on the very same day. Both were named *Green Pastures*, both were for three brothers as owners: the Summers boat for William, Alexander and Albert Ritchie of Inverallochy and the other from the Herd and Mackenzie yard in Buckie for Alexander, John and William Wilson of Portknockie, along with a fourth owner Joseph Gardiner of Cullen.

Malcolm Burge, fisherman, boatbuilder, designer and engineer, amongst other things, on the other hand, came upon a Summers boat more by chance than wishful thinking. He and this partner Kay had just sold a yacht he had in Oban to a fellow from Switzerland and thought they'd like a traditional Scottish fishing boat so that Malcolm could do a spot of fishing as their home is in sight of the waters of the Sound of Mull, on Scotland's west coast. In a moment of inspiration, somewhat regretful in the fullness of time, he judged he'd want something that needed a bit of work doing to her. Consequently, when one popped up on an internet site, this one in Burghead, together they hastened over to view it. Having not yet reached that period of regret, they unsurprisingly not long after found themselves proud owners of the yawl *Amethyst*. She'd been amongst a host of other craft in the harbour there and Malcolm thought this one was worthy. As it turned out she was a bit more worse for wear than he'd initially thought. Nevertheless, living on the west coast, and with the Caledonian Canal closed over the winter of 2015/16, they were able to spend a couple of weeks in Burghead, rewiring the vessel and sorting the worst of the mechanical problems whilst waiting for the canal to open up.

Things weren't helped by the arrival of a Maritime and Coastguard Agency (MCA) surveyor one day, out of the blue. On inspection he judged the boat to be in a dreadful state, giving all manner of reasons in, as is often normal, a tick-box way. However, with some work underway, and a very hectic ensuing twenty-four hours repairing things such as the navigation lights, deck hose and other vital gear, when the surveyor returned the following day, he passed it. Come April, they then spent four days cruising through the canal, down Loch Linnhe and up the Sound of Mull to Lochaline, where the boat is now. By this time any initial thoughts of regret had long disappeared.

Once home, going fishing seemed a good idea but, whilst off the west side of Mull, the Gardner 3LW engine packed up. Sensing dirty fuel, Malcolm got it going once again but realised the obvious: that the fuel tanks were in dire need of replacement. Along with renewing these came a long list of work that was required (and probably a brief bout of being resigned to the project!). Thus he decided the best option was 'to do a proper job', as he put it.

Consequently, over a period of some three years, a list of work as long as your arm was completed by him: new tanks, new wheelhouse, rebuilt engine and gearbox, new winch hydraulics, new net drum, total rewiring, new electronics, new lighting, new top rail and steel handrails. The hull was deemed excellent although he needs to replace the bulwark planking in the future, along with the rudder. The original wooden rudder survives but he says he'd prefer a steel one on a new stainless shaft.

It was interesting to inspect the hull from the inside. The frames were fixed through the hog and keel using iron rivets which Thomas Summers & Co. must have made up. The frames themselves were some 4 x 3in (100 x 75mm) and spaced every 16in (450mm). At the stern it was easy to see the way the cruiser stern was built up from the curved stern piece that was fixed to the sternpost with a huge knee to strengthen it. The frames were then butted onto this. The 1.5in-thick planking was fixed with one rivet in the middle and two dump nails.

Amethyst steaming into Maryport.

Amethyst at Lochaline in November 2018, after rebuilding and with the new wheelhouse. (Courtesy Malcolm Burge)

The forward accommodation, accessible from a deck hatch, was original with two tight berths on the starboard side with storage below, seating along the port side and a new stove against the after bulkhead. Malcolm did mention that after a few days sleeping in the forward one which was the largest, he was keen to get back to a normal bed! Aft of this was the fish room with the engine room at the stern. The new wheelhouse was much further forward than the original pill box type would have been.

A spin out into the Sound of Mull enabled her to show her colours and at 800rpm we easily ran at 6 knots. She rode beautifully and it was easy to see how the Fraserburgh fisherman favoured these yawls. They really are (were) so sea kindly and the only feeling was, when Malcolm turned her around after maybe an hour out, we should have been heading out to sea, not home!

Just down the road from Oban is Crinan, at the west end of the Crinan Canal, where the Summers forty-footer *Excelsior* is to be found today. Originally commissioned by brothers Tommy and Sandy Lawrence, they worked her out of Ballantrae on the Clyde. There's a story about how her Kelvin engine pushed a rod through the hull, the boat being off Ayr, and two boats came to her rescue to raft up alongside and get her home with water pouring in. On decommissioning in 1968, she was sold to Edward H. Gaskins, the owner of a furniture-making factory in Liverpool, to where she was taken by road. It seems she was there for nine years whilst he restored her pretty substantially, even installing a Norwegian hydraulic steering system from a company in Hull. After that, she was sold to Alan Price who finished the internal conversion and fitted the electrics and steel-work on gunwales and winch. He operated her from Liverpool, voyaging as far as the Scilly Isles and Isle of Man with fishing parties and dive charters, undertaking film work as well as wreck and gold hunting with a Magnatron. He then converted her to a family cruiser and sold her to a fellow who kept her in Liverpool and then, in 2001, to Mark and Linda Bowman from Abercalder Bridge, Fort Augustus, on the Caledonian Canal from where she was sold in October 2018.

She was bought up by Rob Walker for the absolute bargain sum of £1. Being close by, I chanced upon a visit in March 2019 when, having viewed *Amethyst* not twenty-four hours earlier, it was interesting to compare construction. Surprisingly, the frame sizes weren't too different. However, the beamshelf on *Excelsior* had an extra smaller one above the main one. A hefty apron at the bow took the forward ends of the planks. At the stern there was no apron, just a very heavy sternpost with a similar stem piece. Everything seemed to be bolted rather than riveted but this could have been a change when she was restored

Excelsior, BA250, lying in the docks at Liverpool prior to restoration. (Courtesy Rob Walker)

Excelsior being carried on a low-loader through the streets of Liverpool. (Courtesy Rob Walker)

at Liverpool in the mid-1990s. Nevertheless the Gardner 6LX sounded good when it was going.

Moored just behind *Excelsior* in the canal basin is the ring-netter *Scarbh*, TT106, built by J. Adam of Gourock in 1947. Although in near-perfect condition, from a visual inspection inside her spacious engine room with her Gardner 6LW, the obvious difference is in the size of the timbers. *Scarbh* exhibited the normal light west coast frames, given the sea conditions where the ringers worked and the necessity of their manoeuvring with the ring-net in confined waters. On the other hand, the boats built for the heavier North Sea were just that: built with hefty bits of oak. That's not to denigrate *Scarbh* and the like as they were built with a different job in mind and just to see the beautiful and nurtured condition of *Scarbh* today says it all in that regard. Nevertheless, it was a useful comparison which simply reinforces my belief that Tommy Summers and his crew were amongst the foremost of fishing-boat builders, in whatever direction you care to look. In Jim McKerracher's words their boats, especially the yawls, 'had style, shape and size'.

Fraserburgh in the late 1960s.

James Noble's yard with its slipway where Thomas Summers & Co. launched their yawls.

The yard with one of the two biggest boats Tommy Summers ever built – either *WFP* or *Ada Kirby* – on the stocks, along with a yawl, thus dating this to 1957/58.

Painting of Tommy Summers by his son Thomas Duncan Summers. (Courtesy Thomas Summers)

The *Fellowship*, ex-*Star of Buchan*, photographed in New Zealand in 2014. (Courtesy Mike Craine)

Girl Helen, INS165.

Shearbill, GY571.

A deck view of *Fortuna*, LK29, with the typical wheelhouse and side pounds.

Star Divine, BF119, against the far wall. I included this photo because of the diversity of the four different sterns on the left of the photo.

Convallaria, BF103, steaming into Fraserburgh past the lighthouse at the end of Balaclava Breakwater, with her whaleback.

Arran Lass, BA168, ex-*Flourish*, FR149, entering Peel. (Courtesy Mike Craine)

Crew aboard *Silver Fern*, FR173, ex-*Gladiolus*, BF255.

Galilean, de-registered but ex-FR136 and SY53, alongside the ringer *Christina*, preparing for the sail across the Atlantic with aid for Honduras, a project that ultimately failed.

The crew of *Excelsior*, BA250, in the late 1950s. L–R: Archie Clery, Tommy Lawrence and Sandy Lawrence. (Courtesy Rob Walker)

Excelsior in Liverpool Docks, late 1960s, when the docks were full of shipping from all over the world. (Courtesy Rob Walker)

Excelsior aboard a Pickfords low-loader on route for conversion with Liverpool's iconic Liver Building in the background. (Courtesy Rob Walker)

Green Pastures, FR37, alongside
Kames pier, Tighnabruaich,
in the summer of 1984,
getting a tidy-up. (Courtesy
Hodgkinson-Cresswell)

Jeannie Stella, RO50, built by
Tommy Summers and Peter
McKichan in 1964.

Postcard from Port Erin with *Harvest Moon*, CT14, lying beached by the short pier.

Winsome, FR45 leaving Fraserburgh on a low-loader, late 1960s. (Courtesy John Alexander Johnston)

Guiding Star, FR31, in Fraserburgh harbour *c.* 1967. Built for James A. Ritchie, in the yellow oilskins hidden from view by his son, also James A. Ritchie and wee grandson Kenneth Ritchie who sent me the photo. Also Eddie Livingstone bending on left. (Courtesy James A. and Fred Ritchie)

Gracious, FR167, ashore.

A good catch of mackerel aboard *Gracious*. (Courtesy AlexanderWest)

Girl Avril, OB372, ex-*Ocean Swell*, in Girvan harbour with a harpoon on the foredeck for hunting basking sharks. (Courtesy Mike Craine)

Venture, BH179, ex-*Girl Avril*, in Blyth in 2009 where she is currently fishing. (Courtesy Stephen Worthington)

Kittiwake, UL128, fishing in sheltered waters.

Kittiwake, UL128, up for a seasonal scrub-up at Waterloo Boatyard, Broadford. She is currently working from Armadale, Sound of Sleat, opposite Mallaig.

Harvest Lily, UL32, in Ullapool some years ago when she was still fishing. Today she's currently afloat but de-registered.

Girl Jane, FR92, now *Fair Morn*, and fishing from Falmouth.

Hopeful, K118, (original PD312) in Kirkwall where she's currently fishing from.

Lenten Rose, FY43 (originally FR92), sailing in Cornish waters where she continues to fish out of Mevagissey, albeit currently for sale, December 2019.

Three Summers stems in Scrabster harbour, late 1960s: *Shamariah*, FR245, *Accord*, FR269, ex-*Edna*, BCK157, and *Harvest Lily*, FR227.

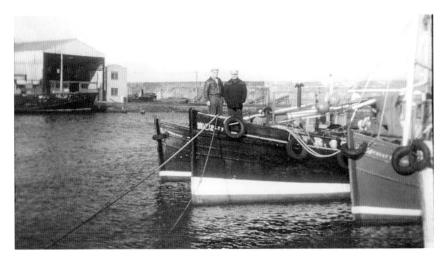

Fraserburgh with the James Noble yard in the background. *Shamariah* on the outside, alongside the Wilson Noble-built Zulu *Violet*, FR451 (built 1911), then *Harvest Lily* and possibly *Valiant* on the inside.

LISTS OF FISHING BOATS BUILT BY THOMAS SUMMERS & CO., FRASERBURGH, BETWEEN 1949 AND 1964

'The human animal differs from the lesser primates in his passion for lists.'
(H. Allen Smith)

7

LIST OF BIG BOATS BUILT
BETWEEN 1949 AND 1962

(Note: The big boats are regarded as being over 47ft LOA (length overall) which were registered for commercial fishing with licences.)

1. *OCEAN GLEANER*, BF600

A sleek-looking *Ocean Gleaner* soon after her transfer to Kilkeel in 1958.

Year Launched:	1950	First Owner:	A. Watt, Gardenstown

Principal Dimensions:	
Length (m)	21.48
Beam (m)	5.97
Depth (m)	2.44
GRT	47.56
Engine	Gardner 6L3B
HP	152

History and Status:
1958: Sold to W.H McBride & others and to Kilkeel and re-registered N125.
1961: Sold to Thomas C. Trimble.

2. *STAR OF BUCHAN*, FR309

The *Fellowship*, ex-*Star of Buchan*, FR400, steaming off Shetland in about 1968, with Gilbert Buchan as skipper and Jim Tait on the extreme right.

Year Launched:	1952	First Owner:	R. Buchan, Fraserburgh

Principal Dimensions:	
Length (m)	21.21
Beam (m)	6.00
Depth (m)	2.71
GRT	52.23
Engine	Kelvin K6
HP	132

History and Status:
1963: Sold to G. Watt, Gardenstown and renamed *Fellowship*, re-registered BF281.
1967: Sold to Gilbert Buchan and re-registered FR400.
1977: Sold to New Zealand and last seen in Auckland.

3. *GLEANER*, FR291

Gleaner, FR291, steaming hard alongside *Victory*.

Year Launched:	1952	First Owner:	W. Duthie, Fraserburgh

Principal Dimensions:	
Length (m)	20.27
Beam (m)	5.73
Depth (m)	2.65
GRT	46.66
Engine	Kelvin K6
HP	132

History and Status:
1960: Wrecked off Shetland.

4. *MORNING STAR*, PD234

Morning Star, PD234.

Year Launched:	1952	First Owner:	G. Duncan, Peterhead

Principal Dimensions:	
Length (m)	23.13
Beam (m)	5.97
Depth (m)	2.74
GRT	75.44
Engine	Gardner 6L3B
HP	152

History and Status:
Re-registered FR286.
1973: Ran ashore and sunk in the Sound of Mull whilst under tow from Tobermory to Oban.

5. *RADIANT WAY*, FR329

Left: *Radiant Way* alongside in Great Yarmouth unloading baskets of herring.
Right: *Radiant Way* showing off her lovely sheer line.

Year Launched:	1952	First Owner:	R. Duthie, Cairnbulg

Principal Dimensions:	
Length (m)	21.43
Beam (m)	5.91
Depth (m)	2.80
GRT	53.65
Engine	Kelvin
HP	132

History and Status:
1966: Wrecked off Stoer Point.
Replaced with *Harvester*, FR22, and renamed *Radiant Way*.

6. *FISHER QUEEN*, FR331

Fisher Queen, FR331.

Year Launched:	1953	First Owner:	F. Blackhall, Fraserburgh

Principal Dimensions:	
Length (m)	20.27
Beam (m)	5.70
Depth (m)	2.65
GRT (m)	46.12
Engine	Gardner 6L3B
HP	152

History and Status:
1966: Sold at auction to Ireland.
1973: Wrecked near Gunna Sound.

7. *RITCHIES*, FR25

Ritchies, FR25, steaming into Great Yarmouth.

Year Launched:	1953	First Owner:	J. Ritchies, Fraserburgh

Principal Dimensions:	
Length (m)	22.22
Beam (m)	6.1
Depth (m)	2.44
GRT	49.39
Engine	Gardner 6L3B
HP	152

History and Status:
Built as a drifter/seiner.
Renamed *Hawthorn*, FR25.
1986: Decommissioned.

8. *LILACINA*, BF395

Lilacina, BF395, the boat that launched a few minutes prematurely!

Year Launched:	1953	First Owner:	W.R. Nicol, Gardenstown

Principal Dimensions:	
Length (m)	19.8
Beam (m)	5.4
Depth (m)	1.9
GRT	47
Engine	Gardner 6L3B
HP	152

History and Status:
1980: Re-registered LH205.
1986: Decommissioned and sold for a house boat.

9. *GIRL HELEN*, INS165

The launch of *Girl Helen*, INS165, off the quayside, creating quite a splash. See how the forefoot scrapes its way down over the stonework of the quay.

Year Launched:	1953	First Owner:	G. Stewart, Lossiemouth

Principal Dimensions:	
Length (m)	19.30
Beam (m)	5.70
Depth (m)	2.44
GRT	40.72
Engine	Gardner 6L3B
HP	152

History and Status:
Renamed *Avalon 2* and re-registered WK343.
1983: Sold to Newlyn and re-registered TH243.
1991: In collision with a tanker in the English Channel.

10. *TUDOR ROSE*, INS284

Tudor Rose after her re-registration as PD7.

Year Launched:	1954	First Owner:	W.J. Farquhar, Lossiemouth

Principal Dimensions:	
Length (m)	18.90
Beam (m)	5.79
Depth (m)	2.56
GRT	42.09
Engine	Gardner 6L3B
HP	152

History and Status:
*c.*1969: Re-registered PD7.
Based in Whitehaven for some time.
1975: Sold to Northern Ireland and became *Tudor Rose*, D615.

11. *WESTHAVEN*, FR375

Westhaven, FR375, in the river Yare at Yarmouth.

Year Launched:	1954	First Owner:	W. Buchan, Fraserburgh

Principal Dimensions:	
Length (m)	22.40
Beam (m)	6.13
Depth (m)	2.74
GRT	56.58
Engine	Gardner 6L3B
HP	152

History and Status:
Renamed *Amoria*, *Clarion*, *Star of Buchan* and *Maranatha*.
1985: Sunk.

12. *GRACEFUL*, FR27

Graceful, FR27, rigged for herring drifting and working.

Year Launched:	1954	First Owner:	J. Buchan, St Combs

Principal Dimensions:	
Length (m)	21.18
Beam (m)	6.03
Depth (m)	2.53
GRT	48.66
Engine	Gardner 6L3B
HP	152

History and Status:
Re-registered LK29.
Transferred to Portavogie and renamed *Be Graceful*, and re-registered B232. Trawled for white fish, prawns and herring.

13. *LUNAR BOW*, PD425

Left: *Lunar Bow*, PD245, with seven crew poised for the camera, preparing to shoot the nets. Right: *Melinka*, ex-*Lunar Bow*, re-registered as FR91 and with new whaleback, steaming into Fraserburgh harbour.

Year Launched:	1954	First Owner:	A. Buchan, Peterhead

Principal Dimensions:	
Length (m)	22.56
Beam (m)	6.16
Depth (m)	2.47
GRT	69.06
Engine	Gardner 6L3B
HP	152

History and Status:
Renamed *Melinka* and re-registered FR81.
Taken to Glengarriff, County Cork, and converted 'extensively' for diving with a hoist said to be on the aft deck. Apparently, she didn't pass a safety test and left Glengarriff, possibly for the Mediterranean.

14. *GIRL MAY*, PD283

Girl May, PD283, steaming out of Peterhead harbour.

Year Launched:	1954	First Owner:	Caledonian Fishselling Co., Peterhead

Principal Dimensions:	
Length (m)	22.20
Beam (m)	4.90
Depth (m)	2.70
GRT	49
Engine	Gardner 6L3B
HP	152

History and Status:
1960: Sold to Robert Tait and re-registered BF204.
1970: Sold to G. Farquhar, Portessie.
1980: Sold to A.H. Bruce.
1985: Sold to M. McSweeney.
1992: Transferred to Ireland, possibly based in Skerries, and re-registered D572 Last seen in Balbriggan.

LAUNCH

OF

M.B. "GIRL MAY"

P.D. 283

★

11th JULY, 1953

Clockwise from above: The launching ceremony of *Girl May*, with the champagne bottle ready. Is that May about to bless the boat, with fishermen and wives looking on?; Another fine photo of *Girl May*; *Girl May* at sea; Cover of *Girl May*'s launch programme; The launch of M.B. *Girl May*.

THE LAUNCH OF M.B. "GIRL MAY," PD. 283.

• • • •

Gently gliding from the builder's cradle bed,
 "Girl May" slips down the ways, so sure and free,
The naming and the words of blessing said,
 Now she floats upon *her* future home—The Sea.

What awaits her in the days that lie before
 None can foresee, but all will wish the best,
That those who own, and those who sail in her
 May find, *she never fails* in any test.

Our blessing and our prayers go with her still,
 Our hopes for her success each coming day,
May He who rules the waves, in His good will
 Stretch out His hand in blessing o'er "Girl May."

M. HANNAH.

15. *NORTHERN VENTURE*, FR14

Left: The long-liner *Northern Venture*, FR14, entering Aberdeen. Right: Sporting a new wheelhouse, *Northern Venture* sank soon after this photo was taken.

Year Launched:	1955	First Owner:	James Summers, St Combs

Principal Dimensions:	
Length (m)	24.62
Beam (m)	6.67
Depth (m)	3.05
GRT	99.80
Engine	Lister Blackstone
HP	220

History and Status:
Built as a great liner, working in northern waters.
1993: Sunk near Baltasound, on the east coast of Unst, Shetland; crew rescued by lifeboat.

16. *PRESENT HELP, FR53*

Present Help, FR53, in Fraserburgh harbour.

Year Launched:	1955	First Owner:	G. Whyte, Fraserburgh

Principal Dimensions:	
Length (m)	21.73
Beam (m)	6.10
Depth (m)	2.53
GRT	50.05
Engine	Gardner 6L3B
HP	152

History and Status:
Sold to Ireland, renamed *Jean Elaine* and re-registered G20.
Converted to a dive boat and last reported working the wrecks of Scapa Flow.

17. *SERENE*, LK63

Serene, LK63, off Shetland.

Year Launched:	1955	First Owner:	M. Polson, Whalsay

Principal Dimensions:	
Length (m)	21.73
Beam (m)	6.03
Depth (m)	2.65
GRT	48.22
Engine	Gardner 6L3B
HP	152

History and Status:
Re-registered BF46, SO647.
1977: Transferred to Ireland and renamed *Scarlet Chord*, B279.
1980: Renamed *Girl May* and transferred to CN240.
1989: Re-registered PD239 and PD788.
1998: Transferred to Portavogie.
2000: Decommissioned.

18. *SURPRISE*, INS11

Left: The launch of *Surprise*, INS11. Right: *Surprise* steaming out past Balaclava Breakwater.

Year Launched:	1955	First Owner:	G. Young, Hopeman

Principal Dimensions:	
Length (m)	16.28
Beam (m)	5.18
Depth (m)	1.98
GRT	24.86
Engine	Gardner 6LW
HP	84

History and Status:
Renamed *Enterprising*.
1994: Decommissioned.

19. *WELFARE*, INS77

Welfare, INS77, about to enter the sea lock of the Caledonian Canal at Corpach on her way out of the canal, with Fort William in the background.

Year Launched:	1955	First Owner:	W. McPherson, Hopeman

Principal Dimensions:	
Length (m)	17.86
Beam (m)	5.55
Depth (m)	2.29
GRT	34.52
Engine	Gardner 6L3B
HP	152

History and Status:
Re-registered BA31.
Transferred to Donaghadee and renamed *Wandering Star*, B21.
Transferred to Scotland (Outer Hebrides) and renamed *Girl Laureen*, SY64.
1996: Scrapped Goat Island, Stornoway.

20. *SCOTTISH MAID*, BF50

Year Launched:	1956	First Owner:	J. Scott, Fraserburgh

Principal Dimensions:	
Length (m)	16.28
Beam (m)	5.18
Depth (m)	1.98
GRT	24.86
Engine	Gardner 6L3B
HP	152

History and Status:
1962: Ran aground, made it to an inlet and sank alongside a jetty near Cape Wrath.

21. *SHEARBILL*, GY571

The first of the Grimsby Danish-style seiners *Shearbill*, GY571, following another similar seiner, *Christen Bank*, GY207.

Year Launched:	1956	First Owner:	Grimsby & Brixham Trawler Company Ltd, Grimsby

Principal Dimensions:	
Length (m)	15.84
Beam (m)	4.97
Depth (m)	1.58
GRT	29.14
Engine	Kelvin K4
HP	88

History and Status:
Transferred to Fleetwood and re-registered FD134.
Transferred to Ayr.
1999: Decommissioned and converted to dive boat, currently in Grimsby.

Shearbill after the hull had been darkened.

Shearbill with a new wheelhouse and rigged for trawling.

22. *MARGARET ROSE*, FR183

Margaret Rose, FR183, off the old seafront at Aberdeen when at the seine net in the late 1950s.

Year Launched:	1956	First Owner:	A. Watt, Fraserburgh

Principal Dimensions:	
Length (m)	21.82
Beam (m)	6.19
Depth (m)	2.83
GRT	57.77
Engine	Gardner 6L3B
HP	152

History and Status:
1960s: Worked the herring pair with *Prevail*.
Renamed *Prospective*, BF400.
1989: Sunk in the Minch, almost halfway between Barra and Hyskeir.

23. MOORHEN, GY593

The second Grimsby seiner *Moorhen*, GY181, in a sorry state in the early 1970s.

Year Launched:	1956	First Owner:	Grimsby & Brixham Trawler Company Ltd, Grimsby

Principal Dimensions:	
Length (m)	15.84
Beam (m)	4.97
Depth (m)	1.58
GRT	29.14
Engine	Kelvin K4
HP	88

History and Status:
1971: Sold to Allard Hewson & Co. Ltd, Grimsby and re-registered GY181.
1975: Sold to Ronald Bond, Fleetwood and re-registered FD306.
1979: Sold to W. H. Gregg & Sons Ltd, Hartlepool and others.
Post 1987: Subsequently converted for pleasure.

24. *NIMROD*, INS4

Nimrod, INS4, in front of the old pontoon in Fraserburgh.

Year Launched:	1956	First Owner:	G. Davidson, Burghead

Principal Dimensions:	
Length (m)	19.81
Beam (m)	5.85
Depth (m)	2.65
GRT	45.59
Engine	Gardner 6L3B
HP:	152

History and Status:
1989: Renamed *Capella*, BCK211.
1993: Transferred to Kilkeel and re-registered CN216.
1996: Transferred to Dingle, County Kerry and renamed *Altair*, T98.

25. *GOLDEN SPINNEY*, WK245

Left: *Golden Spinney*, WK245, leaving Wick harbour. Right: A fine view of *Golden Spinney*, now BF3, steaming out of Fraserburgh, early 1970s.

Year Launched:	1957	First Owner:	J. McKenzie, Wick

Principal Dimensions:	
Length (m)	16.43
Beam (m)	5.00
Depth (m)	2.01
GRT	–
Engine	Gardner 6L3B
HP	152

History and Status:
1970: Sold to G. Walker, Fraserburgh and re-registered BF3.
1976: Sold to G. Cowie and re-registered RO38.
1987: Sold to A.M. Hendy, Cornwall and re-registered PZ17.
1992: Sold to S. Orchard, Porthleven.
Currently lying at Pamphlet Creek, Plymouth as a houseboat.

26. *FRUITFUL VINE*, FR195

Fruitful Vine, FR195, taking to the water in a dramatic way directly off the quay.

Year Launched:	1957	First Owner:	J. Goodbrand, Fraserburgh

Principal Dimensions:	
Length (m)	16.30
Beam (m)	5.00
Depth (m)	2.07
GRT	–
Engine	Mack
HP	120

History and Status:
Renamed *Early Dawn*, OB309, AH177.
1982: Sold to Maryport.
Dredged king scallops until decommissioned.

Fruitful Vine alongside in Fraserburgh harbour.

27. *WFP*, LT310

Left: *WFP*, LT310, the first of the two large trawlers destined for Lowestoft.
Right: Another view of this sidewinder.

Year Launched:	1957	First Owner:	LM Trawlers Ltd, Lowestoft

Principal Dimensions:	
Length (m)	29.57
Beam (m)	7.01
Depth (m)	–
GRT	126
Engine	AK Diesels
HP	300

History and Status:
1976: Sunk in the Mediterranean.

28. *FORTUNA*, LK29

Fortuna, LK29, worked Shetland waters for nearly thirty years.

Year Launched:	1957	First Owner:	T.Stewart, Shetland

Principal Dimensions:	
Length (m)	21.30
Beam (m)	6.10
Depth (m)	2.53
GRT	49.23
Engine	Gardner 6L3B
HP	152

History and Status:
1965: Sold to John Irvin.
1985: Sold to A. Williamson, Whalsay.
1987: Sold to J. Grieve & R. Irvin & Sons Ltd and re-registered BCK120.
1993: Decommissioned at Peterhead.

29. *ADA KIRBY*, LT72

Ada Kirby, LT72, the sister ship to *WFP*, at sea.

Year Launched:	1958	First Owner:	LM Trawlers Ltd, Lowestoft

Principal Dimensions:	
Length (m)	29.57
Beam (m)	7.01
Depth (m)	–
GRT	126
Engine	AK Diesels
HP	300

History and Status:
Re-registered LT72.
1983: Lost.

30. *STAR DIVINE*, BF119

Integrity, BCK39, ex-*Star Divine*, in Blyth.

Year Launched:	1958	First Owner:	J. Murray, Gardenstown

Principal Dimensions:	
Length (m)	18.29
Beam (m)	6.00
Depth (m)	2.59
GRT	40.39
Engine	Gardner 6LX
HP	114

History and Status:
1970: Sold to W. Watt, Fraserburgh and renamed *Star of Faith*, FR45.
1973: Sold to J. & T. Robertson, Findochty and renamed *Integrity*, BCK39.
1993: Decommissioned at Thornbush, Inverness.

31. *CONVALLARIA*, BF103

Convallaria, BF103, soon after her launch.

Year Launched:	1958	First Owner:	A. Ritchie, Gardenstown

Principal Dimensions:	
Length (m)	22.92
Beam (m)	6.31
Depth (m)	2.86
GRT	62.52
Engine	Gardner 6L3B
HP	152

History and Status:
1973: Sold to A. Hepburn, Gardenstown and renamed *Colleague*.
1994: Decommissioned at Fraserburgh.

32. *FAITHFUL*, FR246

Faithful, FR246, coming into Lerwick, July 1967. Her first owner, Stuart Buchan, has a lovely model of her in a bottle. (Courtesy J.A. Hughson)

Year Launched:	1959	First Owner:	Stewart Buchan, Inverallochy

Principal Dimensions:	
Length (m)	16.64
Beam (m)	5.06
Depth (m)	1.98
GRT	24.86
Engine	Gardner 6LX
HP	114

History and Status:
1970: Sold to J. Smith & A. Phimister and renamed *Fragrant Rose*, BCK34.
1976: Sold to J. Reid, Fraserburgh and renamed *Mizpah*, FR223.
1981: Burned out and sank near Oban.

33. *STRATHPEFFER*, BCK95

Strathpeffer, BCK95, moored up alongside at Buckie.

Year Launched:	1959	First Owner:	L. Innes, Portgordon

Principal Dimensions:	
Length (m)	21.61
Beam (m)	5.94
Depth (m)	2.59
GRT	49.75
Engine	Gardner 6L3B
HP	152

History and Status:
1974: Sold to J. Mair, Buckie.
1988: Sold to Kilkeel, Northern Ireland and re-registered N96.
1996: Decommissioned.

34. *WAYFARER*, FR190

The seiner *Wayfarer*, FR190, coming alongside at Lerwick in April 1961, with the island of Bressay in the background. (Courtesy J.A. Hughson)

Year Launched:	1959	First Owner:	A. Wiseman, Macduff

Principal Dimensions:	
Length (m)	19.96
Beam (m)	6.00
Depth (m)	2.71
GRT	48.76
Engine	Gardner 6L3B
HP	152

History and Status:
1967: Sold to A. Wiseman, Macduff and re-registered BF377.
1973: Transferred to H. Anderson, Dunure and re-registered BA377.
1983: Sold to L. Oldman, Banff and re-registered BF25.
1995: Sold to S. Leach, St Ives and re-registered SS252.
2008: Decommissioned at Newlyn and cut up to make sheds. Last Summers big fishing boat.

35. *EMULOUS*, INS93

Left: *Emulous*, INS93, off Aberdeen's old seafront (also seen on page 90).
Right: *Emulous* with a new wheelhouse.

Year Launched:	1959	First Owner:	J. More, Hopeman

Principal Dimensions:	
Length (m)	21.30
Beam (m)	6.16
Depth (m)	2.99
GRT	59.24
Engine	Gardner 6L3B
HP	152

History and Status:
Renamed *Carbreisa*, then *Dorothy D*, A443, ME73.

36. *FLOURISH*, FR149

Left: *Flourish*, FR149, the first Summers launch at the old Wilson Noble yard.
Right: *Vagrant*, LK49, ex-*Flourish*, off Shetland.

Year Launched:	1960	First Owner:	G. Watt, Fraserburgh

Principal Dimensions:	
Length (m)	17.34
Beam (m)	5.46
Depth (m)	2.19
GRT	30.74
Engine	Gardner 6LX
HP	114

History and Status:
Renamed *Vagrant* and re-registered LK45.
Renamed *Arran Lass* and re-registered BA168.
1990: Sold to Portavogie.
1991: Gutted by fire 15 miles off Bradda Head. Port St Mary lifeboat stood by the vessel before *Arran Lass* got a tow home. She was later scrapped.

37. *GIRL WILMA*, INS53

Girl Wilma, INS53, at sea.

Year Launched:	1960	First Owner:	A. McKenzie, Lossiemouth

Principal Dimensions:	
Length (m)	18.04
Beam (m)	5.46
Depth (m)	2.19
GRT	34.71
Engine	Gardner 6LX
HP	114

History and Status:
Renamed *Cairngorm* and re-registered BF53.
Renamed *Girl Claire* and re-registered DO63, B8.
Renamed *Loyalty*.
1992: Sold to England.

38. *EMERALD*, FR289

Emerald, FR289, entering the sea lock of the Caledonian Canal at Corpach.

Year Launched:	1960	First Owner:	N. Downie, Fraserburgh

Principal Dimensions:	
Length (m)	18.71
Beam (m)	6.00
Depth (m)	2.56
GRT	42.52
Engine	Gardner 6L3B
HP	152

History and Status:
Transferred to Kilkeel and re-registered N388.

39. *FERRIBY, GY621*

Left: *Ferriby*, GY621, the last of the Danish-type seiners. (Courtesy Peter H. Pool)
Right: Deck view of *Ferriby*, tragically lost in the North Sea in 1970.

Year Launched:	1960	First Owner:	Grimsby & Brixham Trawler Company Ltd, Grimsby

Principal Dimensions:	
Length (m)	15.84
Beam (m)	4.97
Depth (m)	1.58
GRT	29.14
Engine	Kelvin K4
HP	88

History and Status:
1970: Foundered in the North Sea while fishing out of Grimsby. No survivors.

40. *PROVIDENCE*, FR168

Left: *Providence*, FR168, at Seahouses. Right: *Providence* ashore for a refit.

Year Launched:	1960	First Owner:	T. Dawson, Seahouses

Principal Dimensions:	
Length (m)	15.88
Beam (m)	5.24
Depth (m)	1.92
GRT	23.80
Engine	Gardner 6LX
HP	114

History and Status:
Re-registered LH466, K37, SN36.

41. *QUIET WATERS*, FR253

Quiet waters, FR253, alongside the J. Watt-built *Sincerity*, BF39.

Year Launched:	1960	First Owner:	William Ritchie, Inverallochy

Principal Dimensions:	
Length (m)	16.70
Beam (m)	5.27
Depth (m)	1.92
GRT	24.92
Engine	Gardner 6LX
HP	114

History and Status:
Renamed *Green Castle*, and re-registered BRD179.
Converted as a pleasure vessel.
2019: Ashore on slip at Villa Joyosa, Alicante, Spain.

42. *BDELLIUM*, FR185

Left: *Bdellium*, FR185, in Fraserburgh. Right: Another photo of *Bdellium* in Fraserburgh.

Year Launched:	1961	First Owner:	Frank West, Fraserburgh

Principal Dimensions:	
Length (m)	22.92
Beam (m)	6.16
Depth (m)	1.92
GRT	59.73
Engine	Gardner 6L3B
HP	152

History and Status:
Herring drifter but went to the long-lines at Mallaig and Stranraer outside herring season.
1967: First purse-seiner from Fraserburgh at the herring.
1976: Sold to John Nicol, Gardenstown and renamed *Grateful* and re-registered BF340.
1994: Sold to James Buchan, Inverallochy, renamed *Avail* and re-registered FR194.
1996: Decommissioned at Hull.

43. *GUIDING STAR*, LH382

Left: *Guiding Star*, LH392, alongside at Lerwick, April 1961. (Courtesy J.A. Hughson)
Right: *Guiding Star* steaming out of Aberdeen harbour.

Year Launched:	1961	First Owner:	W. Liston Ltd, Newhaven

Principal Dimensions:	
Length (m)	21.27
Beam (m)	6.00
Depth (m)	2.59
GRT	49.43
Engine	Gardner 6L3B
HP	152

History and Status:
Mid 1960s: Re-registered A777 and working from Aberdeen.
September 1966–October 1967: Spent this time seine netting in Canada, teaching the method to Canadians. Whaleback fitted for transatlantic voyage.
1974: Fishing Shetland.
1975: Sold to Dartmouth and converted for pleasure.

8

LIST OF FORTY-FOOTERS BUILT BETWEEN 1949 AND 1962

Notes:

Forty-footers are considered as being between 37ft and 47ft LOA and registered for commercial fishing with licences.

Two other craft are known to have been built by the yard that are worth listing as it is believed they fitted into this category, though few details are available.

One was a yacht called *Vigilant* built on the lines of a 40ft fishing boat, but with accommodation and a rig for a fellow called Duncan Fletcher. Part of the condition for the commission was that Thomas Summers was to call his next son (if he was to have another child and it was a boy) Duncan Fletcher. He did, naming him Thomas Duncan Fletcher Summers. This was pre-1951 and so was early on in the life of Thomas Summers & Co.

The other was a motor yacht, possibly *Creole*, built for English owners.

1. *GLADIOLUS*, BF255

The same vessel some years later, renamed and re-registered *Galilean*, FR136, with a new winch and radar.

Year Launched:	1951	First Owner:	G. Findlay, Whitehills

Principal Dimensions:	
Length (m)	12.19
Beam (m)	4.42
Depth (m)	1.77
GRT	14.38
Engine	Kelvin K3
HP	66

History and Status:
Renamed *Silver Fern*, FR173, TT93.
Renamed *Galilean*, FR136, SY53.
1999: Sold to England as part of the fleet intended to sail for aid relief in Honduras. Project failed.
2000: Moored up on the river Lynher and subsequently sold and possibly moved to France.

Gladiolus, BF255, leaving Fraserburgh harbour for seining.

2. *SILVER FERN*, BF369

Silver Fern, BF369, alongside Macduff fish market with possibly *Guiding Star*, BF206, and *Endeavour*, BF10, ahead.

Year Launched:	1951	First Owner:	W. Watt, Macduff

Principal Dimensions:	
Length (m)	13.87
Beam (m)	4.78
Depth (m)	1.83
GRT	–
Engine	Gardner 5LW
HP	70

History and Status:
1961: Renamed *Branch* and re-registered FR209.
1963: Sold to J. Criggie, Gourdon and re-registered ME188.
1964: Sold to John Innes, Helmsdale and re-registered WK294.
1972: Sold to D. MacDonald and re-registered UL108.
1973: Re-registered INS.
1974: Sold to J. McIntyre, Barra and re-registered CY93.
1987: Sold to K. Flaws, Lerwick and re-registered LK296.
1990: Decommissioned.

3. HA'BURN, BF269

Ha'burn, BF269, with the Buckie fish market behind.

Year Launched:	1951	First Owner:	J. L. Runcie, Cullen

Principal Dimensions:	
Length (m)	12.19
Beam (m)	4.45
Depth (m)	1.83
GRT	–
Engine	Kelvin K4
HP	88

History and Status:
1970: Sold to Hartlepool and later transferred to A289.
1978: Damaged by ice and sunk in river Dee, raised and taken to Nairn for repair.
Transferred to INS310 working prawn trawl out of Lossiemouth & Burghead.
Transferred to BA170 (BA79).
1989: Caught WW2 mine in net, bomb disposal experts set fuse which detonated early causing hull damage off Great Cumbrae island. Boat beached and crew taken off by lifeboat. Boat submerged but taken to Largs marina and repaired by Navy.
1994: Sold to Greenock.
1997: Put ashore for conversion to pleasure but broken up three years later.

4. *GIRL DOREEN*, PD286

Girl Doreen, PD286, with coils aboard.

Year Launched:	1953	First Owner:	R. Buchan, Peterhead

Principal Dimensions:	
Length (m)	12.07
Beam (m)	4.45
Depth (m)	1.86
GRT	14.83
Engine	Kelvin K3
HP	66

History and Status:
Renamed *Stanhope*, BF123.
Renamed *Lilac*.
Renamed *Sardonyx*, BA223.
Renamed *Vital Spark*, CN223.

5. *EXCELSIOR*, BA250

Year Launched:	1954	First Owner:	Tommy & Sandy Lawrence, Ayr

Principal Dimensions:	
Length (m)	11.28
Beam (m)	4.42
Depth (m)	1.68
GRT	–
Engine	Kelvin K3
HP	66

History and Status:
Fished with seine net and prawn trawl.
c. 1965: Transferred to Wirral.
1968: Decommissioned in Liverpool, hull rebuilt and engine changed to Gardner.
1970: Converted to pleasure by E.H. Gaskin in Liverpool.
Sold to Arran and operated as a dive boat.
2001: Sold to Mark and Linda Bowman.
Purchased by current owners and now based at Crinan.

6. *GREEN PASTURES, FR37*

Green Pastures, FR37, lying in Fraserburgh harbour.

Year Launched:	1954	First Owner:	William Ritchie, Inverallochy

Principal Dimensions:	
Length (m)	12.13
Beam (m)	4.60
Depth (m)	1.95
GRT	16.31
Engine	Gardner 4LW
HP	56

History and Status:
c. 1960: Sold to D. Slater & Co., D.D. Mackay and J. Wiseman, all of Fraserburgh.
1967: Sold to Michael Arthur Hodgkinson of Higher Whitley, Warrington and boat refitted by Forbes summer 1967. Fitted with a new, extended steel casing and new, larger wheelhouse, and accommodation refurbished and improved.
1983: On Hodgkinson's death, partners were R. Williamson and A. Owen of Lymm, Cheshire, and boat put up for sale, lying at Arklow and cared for by Tyrrells boatyard.
1984: Sold to J. Cresswell of Tighnabruaich for sea angling and dive charter work, with some prawn creels and lines rigged for summer spurdog, worked with a portable hauler.
1985: Sold to Katharine Annie Divers and used for sea angling.
1994: Sold to Maryport.
Converted for pleasure with a large deckhouse and, I believe, currently in Whitehaven for sale.

7. *BOY PETER*, PD146

Boy Peter, PD146, with P. Paterson aboard maybe?

Year Launched:	1955	First Owner:	P. Paterson, Peterhead

Principal Dimensions:	
Length (m)	12.07
Beam (m)	4.51
Depth (m)	1.89
GRT	15.65
Engine	Kelvin K3
HP	66

History and Status:
Renamed *Concord*, RO37, CN264.
Renamed *Harvest Gleaner*, TT123.
Renamed *Hollena*, BA42, TT45.
1989: Transferred to Newlyn.

8. *BOY JOHN*, PD140

Boy John, PD140, with coils aboard steaming past Peterhead.

Year Launched:	1955	First Owner:	J. Buchan, Peterhead

Principal Dimensions:	
Length (m)	12.04
Beam (m)	4.57
Depth (m)	1.95
GRT	16.46
Engine	Kelvin K3
HP	66

History and Status:
1973: Transferred to TT84, fished from Whitehaven and Girvan.
1984: Transferred to England.

9. *GRADITUDE*, PD143

Year Launched:	1955	First Owner:	J. McGee, Peterhead

Principal Dimensions:	
Length (m)	12.04
Beam (m)	4.51
Depth (m)	1.92
GRT	15.86
Engine	Kelvin K3
HP	66

History and Status:
Renamed *Brighter Morn*, CN72.
Renamed Speedwell.
1987: Transferred to England.

10. *ILLUSTRIOUS*, PD169

Illustrious with her first forward wheelhouse conversion.

Year Launched:	1955	First Owner:	W. Mair, Peterhead

Principal Dimensions:	
Length (m)	12.07
Beam (m)	4.51
Depth (m)	2.16
GRT	–
Engine	Kelvin K3
HP	66

History and Status:
Transferred to BF345, UL200, K616.
2010: Fishing out of Orkney with forward wheelhouse.
2019: Sold to Portavogie.

11. *BRIGHTER HOPE*, PD155

Brighter Hope, PD155.

Year Launched:	1956	First Owner:	P. Duthie, Peterhead

Principal Dimensions:	
Length (m)	12.07
Beam (m)	4.54
Depth (m)	1.92
GRT	17.35
Engine	Gardner 5LW
HP	72

History and Status:
Renamed *Shonmora*, LH147, TT147.
Renamed *Sean Og*.

12. *WATCHFUL*, PD269

Watchful, PD269.

Year Launched:	1958	First Owner:	A. Buchan, Peterhead

Principal Dimensions:	
Length (m)	12.16
Beam (m)	4.57
Depth (m)	1.89
GRT	15.32
Engine	Gardner 6LW
HP	84

History and Status:
Transferred to INS9, OB39.
Renamed *Glen Carradale*, CN90.
1970: Transferred to England.
2019: Abandoned and sunk at Fleetwood.

13. *SUMMER ROSE*, PD341

Summer Rose, PD341, alongside at Burghead. The frontage, although modernised, still looks the same today as it did fifty years ago.

Year Launched:	1960	First Owner:	J. Buchan, Peterhead

Principal Dimensions:	
Length (m)	12.16
Beam (m)	4.54
Depth (m)	1.86
GRT	84
Engine	Gardner 6LW
HP	84

History and Status:
Transferred to CN141.
Renamed *Heather Joy*, KY118, CN141, TT142.
Renamed *Summer Rose*, BH21, LH290.
Currently ashore at Port Penrhyn, Bangor, under conversion to liveaboard.

14. JANET, FR166

Left: *Janet*, FR166, steaming into Bridlington on a fresh day. (Courtesy Chris Traves)
Right: *St. David*, FR166, ex-*Janet*, on the slip at Rye in 1972, soon after being sold by
George Traves to Stan Pepper, with RX338 astern. (Courtesy Dave Pepper)

Year Launched:	1962	First Owner:	George Traves, Bridlington

Principal Dimensions:	
Length (m)	10.97
Beam (m)	4.11
Depth (m)	1.83
GRT	–
Engine	Kelvin K3
HP	66

History and Status:
Built for potting and lining and named after owner's daughter.
1960s: Converted for trawling.
1972: Sold to Stan Pepper of Rye and renamed *St David*, FR166.
1973: Larger wheelhouse fitted.
Late 1980s: Re-registered RX31.
Currently languishing at Rye as a houseboat.

9

LIST OF YAWLS BUILT
BETWEEN 1949 AND 1962

Notes:

Yawls are considered by many to be the finest craft to emerge from the yard and are regarded as being under 37ft LOA and registered for commercial fishing with licences.

There is also a boat called *Kathleen* that is thought to have been a yawl but no details are available.

1. *FISHER BOYS*, FR54

Year Launched:	1949	First Owner:	J. Duthie, Sandhaven

Principal Dimensions:	
Length (m)	10.36
Beam (m)	3.54
Depth (m)	1.58
GRT	8.66
Engine	Kelvin J3
HP	33

History and Status:
Fisher Boys, UL39, INS243.
1974: Decommissioned.

2. *DAISY*, FR78

A good deck view of *Daisy* in Fraserburgh harbour.

Year Launched:	1949	First Owner:	J. Stephen, Cairnbulg

Principal Dimensions:	
Length (m)	9.39
Beam (m)	3.54
Depth (m)	1.58
GRT	8.36
Engine	Kelvin J3
HP	33

History and Status:
1992: Lost in Cruden Bay not long after a refit.

3. *JUST REWARD*, FR117

Year Launched:	1950	First Owner:	G. Duthie, Fraserburgh

Principal Dimensions:	
Length (m)	10.21
Beam (m)	3.54
Depth (m)	1.52
GRT	7.91
Engine	Kelvin J3
HP	33

History and Status:
Just Reward, BF265, ME37, AH137, PD278.
1993: Transferred to Wick.
1990s: Restored by Jim McKerracher and then re-registered as SY798.
Lost off Ireland.

4. *HARVEST MOON*, FR131

Harvest Moon, FR131, under construction.

Year Launched:	1950	First Owner:	W. Third, Fraserburgh

Principal Dimensions:	
Length (m)	10.88
Beam (m)	3.47
Depth (m)	1.62
GRT	9.51
Engine	Kelvin J4
HP	44

History and Status:
Transferred to the Isle of Man and re-registered CT14.
Transferred to Donaghadee and re-registered BT146.
Renamed *Ingrid Rosa*, SA331.

5. *VIRTUOUS*, FR353

A great shot of *Virtuous*, PD49, on the slip after her sale to Peterhead.

Year Launched:	1953	First Owner:	Jimmy and Alex West, Fraserburgh

Principal Dimensions:	
Length (m)	9.42
Beam (m)	3.41
Depth (m)	1.28
GRT	5.89
Engine	Bolinder
HP	35

History and Status:
Re-registered PD330.
Renamed *Jenna Louise*, UL78.
Renamed back to *Virtuous*, INS40, PD49 & A649.
Converted to a pleasure craft and now lying ashore alongside the owner's house at Skarfskerry, Caithness, where she's been for a couple of decades or more.

6. *EASTER MORN*, FR372

Boy Alec, PD414, ex-*Easter Morn*, FR372, with forward wheelhouse after her rebuild from storm damage.

Year Launched:	1953	First Owner:	A. Duthie, Fraserburgh

Principal Dimensions:	
Length (m)	9.45
Beam (m)	3.50
Depth (m)	1.50
GRT	7.43
Engine	Kelvin J2
HP	22

History and Status:
1959: Wrecked on the beach after the October northerly gale that had sprung up after an unusually calm morning. Andrew Duthie (50) from Inverallochy was drowned. Boat later recovered.
Renamed *Boy Alec*, PD414, UL114.
Currently laid up on beach in Loch Broom opposite Ullapool and probably past restoration.

7. *GOLDEN LILY*, FR21

Golden Lily, FR21, with small shelter, or dodger, aft and fish boxes.

Year Launched:	1954	First Owner:	A. Ritchie, Fraserburgh

Principal Dimensions:	
Length (m)	9.75
Beam (m)	3.54
Depth (m)	1.52
GRT	7.65
Engine	Kelvin J2
HP	22

History and Status:
BRD25, OB58, UL117.
Currently fishing out of Blyth as *Golden Lily*, BH115.

8. *WINSOME*, FR45

Winsome, FR45, lying alongside in the foreground at Fraserburgh, with *Carolanne*, SH175, adjacent.

Year Launched:	1955	First Owner:	W. Buchan, Cairnbulg

Principal Dimensions:	
Length (m)	9.88
Beam (m)	3.54
Depth(m)	1.43
GRT	7.36
Engine	Kelvin J2
HP	22

History and Status:
1969: Sunk on mooring off Ardwell.

9. *GUIDING STAR*, FR31

Left: *Guiding Star* steaming out of Fraserburgh. (Courtesy James A. and Fred Ritchie)
Right: *Guiding Star* alongside. (Courtesy James A. and Fred Ritchie)

Year Launched:	1955	First Owner:	J. Ritchie, Fraserburgh

Not to be confused with the last big boat T. Summers & Co. built, Guiding Star, *LH382, in 1961*

Principal Dimensions:	
Length (m)	9.57
Beam (m)	3.60
Depth(m)	1.52
GRT	7.7
Engine	Kelvin J2
HP	22

History and Status:
It is said that, during construction, Tommy Summers and the skipper of a particular boat being built at the same time as this one fell out over the speed of building this other vessel. One night this skipper came and knocked out the shores holding the frames of *Guiding Star* upright and so delayed its building in the hope that progress would quicken on his commissioned boat.
Re-registered as PD34, then ME34.
Last reported in the Clyde and up for sale.

10. *SCEPTRE*, FR237

Sceptre, BRD173, whilst fishing on the west coast.

Year Launched:	1956	First Owner:	A. Duthie, Fraserburgh

Principal Dimensions:	
Length (m)	9.75
Beam (m)	3.47
Depth (m)	1.52
GRT	7.75
Engine	Kelvin J2
HP	22

History and Status:
Built under WFA grant and loan scheme, line fishing with three crew.
1962: Change of owner to P. Geddes of Fraserburgh.
1966: Change of owner to A. Patrick of Shieldaig and transferred to Kyle district, re-registered BRD173.
1967: Change of owner to Duncan Beaton of Kyle and change of fishing method to creels.
1967: Change of owner to James Matheson of Kyle of Lochalsh.
1973: Change of engine to 62 HP Kelvin.
1979: Change of owner to Grant of Aultbea, Ross-shire and transferred to Ullapool district.
1985: Sold to Northern Ireland and renamed *Graceful Morn*, B172.
Partially restored by Jim McKerracher, Port Penryhn, Bangor and sold on.

11. *GRACIOUS*, FR167

Left: *Gracious*, FR167, powering through the water. Right: *Gracious*.

Year Launched:	1957	First Owner:	Alex West, Fraserburgh

Principal Dimensions:	
Length (m)	10.15
Beam (m)	3.44
Depth (m)	1.43
GRT	7.03
Engine	Russell Newbery
HP	33

History and Status:
1998: Sold to Gilbert Buchan of Killibegs, Ireland and converted to pleasure.
Re-registered as G227 and currently fishing from Rosroe Pier, Killary, County Galway.

12. *GOLDEN QUEST*, FR80

Golden Quest as the Fraserburgh pilot boat before being converted back to fishing.

Year Launched:	1957	First Owner:	G. Watt, Fraserburgh

Principal Dimensions:	
Length (m)	10.15
Beam (m)	3.44
Depth (m)	1.43
GRT	7.03
Engine	Bolinder
HP	35

History and Status:
Became Fraserburgh pilot boat.
Saturn, UL321.
Osprey, LKL321.
Currently fishing as *Lowra May*, LK213, out of Scalloway.

13. *BE IN TIME*, FR64

Be In Time, FR64, with Johnny Strachan and his brother-in-law, Andrew Strachan who was in the Salvation Army, pointing with Dod Love on the far left. As the hymn goes: 'Be in time, be in time, While the voice of Jesus calls you, be in time. If in sin you longer wait, You may find no open gate, And your cry be just too late, be in time.'

Year Launched:	1957	First Owner:	A. Strachan, Inverallochy

Principal Dimensions:	
Length (m)	9.75
Beam (m)	3.41
Depth (m)	1.46
GRT	7.32
Engine	Kelvin J2
HP	22

History and Status:
Named after Salvation Army hymn 'Be In Time', creel and lines.
Re-registered WK420.
1983: Renamed *Be In Time*, OB275, owner B. Langford, rigged for trawling BA275.

14. *GIRL BETTY*, FR219

Girl Betty, LK543, after transferring to Burrafirth, Shetland.

Year Launched:	1957	First Owner:	W. Buchan, Fraserburgh

Principal Dimensions:	
Length (m)	9.75
Beam (m)	3.44
Depth (m)	1.46
GRT	7.32
Engine	Kelvin J3
HP	33

History and Status:
1957: Launched at the time of a nationwide strike in shipyards, she was described as a 'boat in a thousand' by the local newspaper *Press & Journal*. Although the workforce was on strike in the yard, the partners and apprentices worked hard to get her ready for launch on time.
1962: Fishing method changed to shell fishing.
1964: New engine installed: Lister 42 HP.
1969: Transferred to Gibby Fraser of Burrafirth, Shetland for creeling and re-registered LK543.
1970: Transferred to G. Williamson of Skerries; fishing method changed to escallops.
1977: Transferred to Donald C. Mackay of Thurso and re-registered WK185.
1978: Transferred to James Broadant of Thurso.
1982: Vessel took fire and was lost at sea, 3 July 1982.

15. *OCEAN SWELL*, FR69

Girl Avril, BA133, ex-*Ocean Swell*, after transfer to the west coast.

Year Launched:	1958	First Owner:	G. Masson, Sandhaven

Principal Dimensions:	
Length (m)	9.88
Beam (m)	3.47
Depth (m)	1.46
GRT	7.44
Engine	Gardner 3LW
HP	42

History and Status:
Capsized and righted herself; found drifting off Aberdeen a few days after the October 1959 gale and towed in.
Renamed *Girl Avril*, FR69.
Renamed *Ocean Swell*, OB372, BA133.
Renamed *Girl Avril*, BA133, A372.
1990s: Restored by Jim McKerracher, Port Penryhn, Bangor.
Renamed *Venture*, BRD179, BH179 and currently fishing out of Blyth.

16. *MORNING STAR*, FR47

Year Launched:	1958	First Owner:	G. Strachan, Inverallochy

Principal Dimensions:	
Length (m)	10.15
Beam (m)	3.44
Depth (m)	1.46
GRT	7.32
Engine	Kelvin J3
HP	33

History and Status:
Boat was lost off Cairnbulg during the gale of 27 October 1959, with two lives from the Invercairn community being sadly taken: William Strachan (49) from Cairnbulg and Andrew Duthie (62) from Inverallochy.

17. *KITTIWAKE*, UK128

Kittiwake, UL128.

Year Launched:	1958	First Owner:	H. MacDonald, Drumbeg

Principal Dimensions:	
Length (m)	10.15
Beam (m)	3.50
Depth (m)	1.55
GRT	–
Engine	Gardner 4LW
HP	56

History and Status:
Built under WFA grant and loan scheme.
1978: Fitted with a new engine.
1989: Transferred to Oban for nephrop trawl, new owners were Charles Main and Alex Smith.
Currently fishing from Armadale, Sound of Sleat, opposite Mallaig.

18. *HARVEST LILY*, FR227

Harvest Lily, FR227, steaming along.

Year Launched:	1958	First Owner:	W. Buchan, Fraserburgh

Principal Dimensions:	
Length (m)	10.10
Beam (m)	3.47
Depth (m)	1.47
GRT	7.11
Engine	Kelvin J2
HP	22

History and Status:
1973: Transferred to UL32.
Now under private ownership, de-registered at Ullapool, but still sailing.

19. *GIRL JANE*, FR92

Fair Morn, PD224, ex-*Girl Jane*, in Peterhead.

Year Launched:	1959	First Owner:	A. Buchan, Inverallochy

Principal Dimensions:	
Length (m)	10.15
Beam (m)	3.55
Depth (m)	1.58
GRT	8.47
Engine	Gardner 3LW
HP	42

History and Status:
Sold to Peterhead and renamed *Fair Morn*, PD224.
Converted for pleasure in Skye.
Re-registered FH29 and currently fishing from Falmouth as *Fair Morn*.

20. *HOPEFUL*, PD312

Hopeful, PD312, alongside and unloading at Peterhead fish market. Various other yawls are there but no more from Thomas Summers & Co.

Year Launched:	1959	First Owner:	J. Buchan, Peterhead

Principal Dimensions:	
Length (m)	10.67
Beam (m)	3.93
Depth (m)	1.52
GRT	9.72
Engine	Lister
HP	42

History and Status:
Renamed *Lily 2*, FR323, SY79, WK42.
Renamed *Hopeful*, WK455, UL190. Worked from St Ives for a time.
Currently fishing as *Hopeful*, K118, from Stronsay.

21. *LENTEN ROSE*, FR90

Year Launched:	1959	First Owner:	A. Buchan, Fraserburgh

Principal Dimensions:	
Length (m)	10.12
Beam (m)	3.47
Depth (m)	1.52
GRT	7.21
Engine	Bolinder
HP	36

History and Status:
Fished out of Swansea and then Brixham in mid-1980s.
Currently fishing as FY43 out of Mevagissey and for sale.

22. *BOY JAMES*, FR83

Renamed *Reaper*, WK83,
and based at Keiss.

Year Launched:	1959	First Owner:	Unknown

Principal Dimensions:	
Length (m)	10.03
Beam (m)	3.51
Depth (m)	–
GRT	–
Engine	–
HP:	–

History and Status:
Original information scarce.
Renamed *Reaper*, WK83, and fishing from Keiss.
Renamed *Boy James*, FD283.
Renamed *Lindeadar*, BA288.
Decommissioned 1998.

23. *AMETHYST*, FR321

Amethyst, FR321, heading in to catch the market at Fraserburgh, with George Noble washing down the cod. (Courtesy S. Noble)

Year Launched:	1960	First Owner:	A. Noble, Fraserburgh

Principal Dimensions:	
Length (m)	10.15
Beam (m)	3.50
Depth (m)	1.55
GRT	8.21
Engine	Gardner 3LW
HP	42

History and Status:
1970: Berwick.
1984: Workington.
Transferred to Oban, re-registered OB456.
1988: Transferred to J. Clark, Maryport.
1998: Transferred to 'Shaun McG'.
2002: Transferred to Killibegs, re-registered B456.
2015: Transferred to A. Cormie, Burghead, re-registered INS9 and rigged for trawling.
2016: Transferred to J. Mcleod, Burghead.
2017: Transferred to M. Burge, Lochaline and currently fishing.

24. *GRATEFUL*, FR270

Grateful, A753, after her transfer to Stonehaven.

Year Launched:	1960	First Owner:	Willie Sutherland, Fraserburgh

Principal Dimensions:	
Length (m)	10.36
Beam (m)	3.57
Depth(m)	1.49
GRT	8.31
Engine	Gardner 3LW
HP	42

History and Status:
Sold to David Cargill of Stonehaven c. mid–1960s and re-registered A753.
Renamed *San Ray*, A753.
By 1992 she was working from Garlieston as *Loyalty*, A753, with the wheelhouse moved forward. Possibly subsequently decommissioned.

25. *VALIANT*, FR231

Valiant on the Fraserburgh pontoon with the Summers build *Quiet Waters* ahead

Year Launched:	1960	First Owner:	D. Sim, Fraserburgh

Principal Dimensions:	
Length (m)	9.97
Beam (m)	3.54
Depth (m)	1.49
GRT	7.88
Engine	Bolinder
HP	36

History and Status:
Transferred to England in 1972 and later converted for pleasure and renamed *Blue Max*.

26. *BRILLIANT*, BF208

Brilliant, BF208, with the Whitehills seiner *Boy David*, BF361, inside. Sometimes called Radio Luxembourg, after the pirate radio station which operated on 208m Medium Wave and was listened to by many young lads (including the author!). They played music from 7 p.m. to 2 a.m. every night and the last record played before the station closed for the night was 'At the end of the Day', which was played for many years. According to Gilbert Smith: 'I can still hear it to this day. It goes like this: "At the end of the day we kneel and pray and thank you Lord for our work and play". It was a beautiful song to listen to because back then you thought it would never end, but sadly it did for me. That was fifty-eight years ago. Hope this helps you to solve why the *Brilliant*, BF208, was also called Radio Luxembourg.'

Year Launched:	1960	First Owner:	W. Smith, Portsoy

Principal Dimensions:	
Length (m)	10.15
Beam (m)	3.47
Depth (m)	1.46
GRT	7.63
Engine	Gardner 3LW
HP	42

History and Status:
c. 1970: Owner George Slater, Cullen.
c. 1974: Re-registered WK118.
1980s: Re-registered LK1.
1989: Re-registered SY306 based in Berneray, North Uist.
1991: Re-registered K210 based in Stromness.
Currently lying ashore at Sandwick, Shetland as bare hull with no deck. Owner intends to restore her.

27. *EDNA*, BCK157

Left: *Accord*, FR269, helping with the launch of *Fairweather III*, PD197, in 1965 at the Sandhaven yard of J.G. Forbes, along with *Dauntless Star*, PD84, also built by Forbes in 1949. Right: *Accord*, FR269, ex-*Edna*, BCK157, alongside the Malakoff Pier, Lerwick, soon after the launch at Forbes, after being sold to J.W. Smith. At the pier she had some work and modifications done prior to starting her life as a creel boat.

Year Launched:	1961	First Owner:	C. Bruce, Inverallochy

Principal Dimensions:	
Length (m)	10.15
Beam (m)	3.50
Depth (m)	1.52
GRT	8.00
Engine	Gardner 3LW
HP	42

History and Status:
Renamed *Accord*, FR269.
1965: Sold to J.W. Smith as re-registered LK688, working as creel boat.
1967/68: Sold to Edwin Groat and re-registered K932. Wheelhouse shifted forward. After several owners, she became WK165.
Last owner was Sir Patrick Grant of Dalvey who fished prawns with her as UL20. She was damaged during a gale while tied to a pier somewhere on the west coast and later on, while being towed to have this damage repaired, she began to take in water and sank in the Kylesku area.

28. *SHAMARIAH*, FR245

Shamariah, FR245.

Year Launched:	1961	First Owner:	J Buchan, Fraserburgh

Principal Dimensions:	
Length (m)	10.15
Beam (m)	3.50
Depth (m)	1.52
GRT	8.06
Engine	Gardner 3LW
HP	42

History and Status:
*c.*1963: Owned by Jimmy West.
Renamed and re-registered *Sadie Joan*, LK987, and currently fishing.

29. *DAYBREAK*, FR250

Daybreak, FR250, with Andrew Ritchie standing by wheelhouse aft.

Year Launched:	1962	First Owner:	A. Buchan, Fraserburgh

Principal Dimensions:	
Length (m)	10.39
Beam (m)	3.57
Depth (m)	1.31
GRT	7.24
Engine	Lister
HP	34

History and Status:
One of the last finished at the yard and it has said that the yard foreman finished her off before launching. Has been mentioned as a sister ship to *Edna*, although dimensions are only similar.
1979: Transferred to Ramsey, Isle of Man and re-registered RY39.
Won the Manx Trawler Race in the 1980s.
Re-registered SY29, Renamed *Redfin*, TN4.
Renamed *Daybreak*, B129.
Wrecked in gale at Holyhead Marina in 2018.

30. *SPEEDWELL*, FR316

Year Launched:	1962	First Owner:	R. Third, Fraserburgh

Principal Dimensions:	
Length (m)	9.75
Beam (m)	3.66
Depth (m)	1.46
GRT	7.83
Engine	Lister
HP	21

History and Status:
Build finished off by James Nobles Renamed *Thalassa*, FR316.
Renamed *Morning Star*, BRD138, LK.
Moved to Amble and then to Gosport.
Now in Port Penryhn, Bangor under restoration by Jim McKerracher.

31. *BOYNE VALE*, BF266

Year Launched:	1962	First Owner:	J. Smith

Principal Dimensions:	
Length (m)	10.12
Beam (m)	3.55
Depth (m)	1.43
GRT	7.44
Engine	Gardner 3LW
HP	42

History and Status:
2000: Based in Barrow-in-Furness.
2005: Based in Whitehaven.
2009: Transferred to Kilkeel and re-registered N291, later AR1.
Renamed and re-registered *Integrity*, CO830 and currently fishing.
2019: Currently for sale.

APPENDICES

APPENDIX A: PLN NAME CHANGES FOR SUMMERS VESSELS

Home

Tommy Summers PLN & name change reference

Big boat list

PLN	New Name	Launch Name	PLN	PLN	New Name	Launch Name	PLN	PLN	New Name	Launch Name	PLN
A443	Dorothy D	Emulous	INS93	FR194	Avail	Bdellium	FR185	PD788	Girl May	Serene	LK63
A777	Guiding Star	Guiding Star	LH382	FR195	Fruitful Vine	Fruitful Vine	FR195	PZ17	Golden Spinney	Golden Spinney	WK245
B8	Girl Clair	Girl Wilma	INS53	FR223	Mizpah	Faithful	FR246	RO38	Golden Spinney	Golden Spinney	WK245
B21	Wandering Star	Welfare	INS77	FR246	Faithful	Faithful	FR246	SN36	Providence	Providence	FR168
B279	Scarlet Cord	Serene	LK63	FR253	Quiet Waters	Quiet Waters	FR253	SO647	Serene	Serene	LK63
B232	Be Graceful	Graceful	FR27	FR286	Morning Star	Morning Star	PD234	SS252	Wayfarer	Wayfarer	FR190
B279	Scarlet Cord	Serene	LK63	FR289	Emerald	Emerald	FR289	SY64	Girl Laureen	Welfare	INS77
BA168	Arran Lass	Flourish	FR149	FR291	Gleaner	Gleaner	FR291	T88	Altair	Nimrod	INS4
BA317	Welfare	Welfare	INS77	FR309	Star of Buchan	Star of Buchan	FR309	TH243	Avalon 2	Girl Helen	INS165
BA377	Wayfarer	Wayfarer	FR190	FR329	Radiant Way	Radiant Way	FR329	WK245	Golden Spinney	Golden Spinney	WK245
BCK34	Faithful	Faithful	FR246	FR331	Fisher Queen	Fisher Queen	FR331	WK343	Avalon 2	Girl Helen	INS165
BCK39	Integrity	Star Devine	BF119	FR375	Westhaven	Westhaven	FR375				
BCK120	Fortuna	Fortuna	LK29	FR375	Clarion	Westhaven	FR375		**Alphabetical order**		
BCK95	Strathpeffer	Strathpeffer	BCK95	FR375	Star of Buchan	Westhaven	FR375		New Name	Launch Name	PLN	Year
BCK211	Capella	Nimrod	INS4	FR375	Maranatha	Westhaven	FR375		Altair	Nimrod	INS4	1957
BF3	Golden Spinney	Golden Spinney	WK245	FR375	Amoria	Westhaven	FR375		Amoria	Westhaven	FR375	1954
BF25	Wayfarer	Wayfarer	FR190	FR400	Fellowship	Star of Buchan	FR309		Arran Lass	Flourish	FR149	1960
BF46	Serene	Serene	LK63	G20	Jean Elaine	Present Help	FR53		Avail	Bdellium	FR185	1961
BF50	Scottish Maid	Scottish Maid	BF50	GY571	Shearbill	Shearbill	GY571		Avalon 2	Girl Helen	INS165	1953
BF53	Cairngorm	Girl Wilma	INS53	GY593	Moorhen	Moorhen	GY593		Be Graceful	Graceful	FR27	1954
BF53	Loyalty	Girl Wilma	INS53	GY621	Ferniby	Ferniby	GY621		Cairngorm	Girl Wilma	INS53	1960
BF103	Convallaria	Convallaria	BF103	INS4	Nimrod	Nimrod	INS4		Capella	Nimrod	INS4	1957
BF103	Colleague	Convallaria	BF103	INS11	Surprise	Surprise	INS11		Carbreisa	Emulous	INS93	1959
BF119	Star Devine	Star Devine	BF119	INS11	Enterprising	Surprise	INS11		Clarion	Westhaven	FR375	1954
BF204	Girl May	Girl May	PD283	INS53	Girl Wilma	Girl Wilma	INS53		Colleague	Convallaria	BF103	1958
BF281	Fellowship	Star of Buchan	FR309	INS77	Welfare	Welfare	INS77		Dorothy D	Emulous	INS93	1959
BF340	Grateful	Bdellium	FR185	INS93	Emulous	Emulous	INS93		Early Dawn	Fruitful Vine	FR195	1957
BF377	Wayfarer	Wayfarer	FR190	INS93	Carbreisa	Emulous	INS93		Enterprising	Surprise	INS11	1955
BF400	Prospective	Margaret Rose	FR183	INS165	Girl Helen	Girl Helen	INS165		Girl Clair	Girl Wilma	INS53	1960
BF600	Ocean Gleaner	Ocean Gleaner	N125	INS284	Tudor Rose	Tudor Rose	INS284		Girl Laureen	Welfare	INS77	1955
BRD179	Green Castle	Quiet Waters	FR253	K37	Providence	Providence	FR168		Girl May	Serene	LK63	1955
CN240	Girl May	Serene	LK63	LH382	Guiding Star	Guiding Star	LH382		Grateful	Bdellium	FR185	1961
D572	Girl May	Girl May	PD283	LH466	Providence	Providence	FR168		Green Castle	Quiet Waters	FR253	1960
DO63	Girl Clair	Girl Wilma	INS53	LK29	Graceful	Graceful	FR27		Hawthorn	Ritches	FR25	1953
FD134	Shearbill	Shearbill	GY571	LK29	Fortuna	Fortuna	LK29		Integrity	Star Devine	BF119	1958
FD306	Moorhen	Moorhen	GY593	LK45	Vagrant	Flourish	FR149		Jean Elaine	Present Help	FR53	1955
FR14	Northern Venture	Northern Venture	FR14	LK63	Serene	Serene	LK63		Loyalty	Girl Wilma	INS53	1960
FR25	Ritches	Ritches	FR25	LT72	Ada Kirby	Ada Kirby	LT72		Maranatha	Westhaven	FR375	1954
FR27	Graceful	Graceful	FR27	LT310	WFP	WFP	LT310		Melinka	Lunar Bow	PD425	1954
FR53	Present Help	Present Help	FR53	ME76	Dorothy D	Emulous	INS93		Mizpah	Faithful	FR246	1959
FR81	Melinka	Lunar Bow	PD425	N125	Ocean Gleaner	Ocean Gleaner	BF600		Prospective	Margaret Rose	FR183	1956
FR85	Star of Faith	Star Devine	BF119	N388	Emerald	Emerald	FR289		Scarlet Cord	Serene	LK63	1955
FR149	Flourish	Flourish	FR149	OB309	Early Dawn	Fruitful Vine	FR195		Star of Buchan	Westhaven	FR375	1954
FR168	Providence	Providence	FR168	PD7	Tudor Rose	Tudor Rose	INS284		Star of Faith	Star Devine	BF119	1958
FR183	Margaret Rose	Margaret Rose	FR183	PD234	Morning Star	Morning Star	PD234		Vagrant	Flourish	FR149	1960
FR185	Bdellium	Bdellium	FR185	PD239	Girl May	Serene	LK63		Wandering Star	Welfare	INS77	1955
FR190	Wayfarer	Wayfarer	FR190	PD283	Girl May	Girl May	PD283					
				PD425	Lunar Bow	Lunar Bow	PD425					

Tommy Summers PLN & name change reference

40ft boat list

PLN	New Name	Launch Name	PLN		PLN	New Name	Launch Name	PLN
A269	Ha'burn	Ha'burn	BF286		TT147	Shonmora	Brighter Hope	PD155
BA42	Hollena	Boy Peter	PD146		TT147	Sean Og	Brighter Hope	PD155
BA79	Ha'burn	Ha'burn	BF286		TT277	Jeannie Stella	Jeannie Stella	RO50
BA223	Sardonyx	Girl Doreen	PD286		UL108	Branch	Silver Fern	BF369
BA250	Excelsior	Excelsior	BA250		UL200	Illustrious	Illustrious	PD169
BF123	Stanhope	Girl Doreen	PD286		WK294	Branch	Silver Fern	BF369
BF123	Lilac	Girl Doreen	PD286					
BF255	Gladiolus	Gladiolus	BF255			**Alphabetical order**		
BF286	Ha'burn	Ha'burn	BF286			New Name	Launch Name	PLN	Year
BF345	Illustrious	Illustrious	PD169			Boy John	Boy John	PD140	1955
BF369	Silver Fern	Silver Fern	BF369			Boy Peter	Boy Peter	PD146	1955
BH21	Summer Rose	Summer Rose	PD341			Branch	Silver Fern	BF369	1951
CN72	Brighter Morn	Gratitude	PD143			Brighter Hope	Brighter Hope	PD155	1956
CN72	Speedwell	Gratitude	PD143			Brighter Morn	Gratitude	PD143	1955
CN90	Glen Carradale	Watchful	PD269			Concord	Boy Peter	PD146	1955
CN141	Summer Rose	Summer Rose	PD341			Excelsior	Excelsior	BA250	1954
CN223	Vital Spark	Girl Doreen	PD286			Galilean	Gladiolus	BF255	1951
CN264	Concord	Boy Peter	PD146			Girl Doreen	Girl Doreen	PD286	1953
CY93	Branch	Silver Fern	BF369			Gladiolus	Gladiolus	BF255	1951
FR37	Green Pastures	Green Pastures	FR37			Glen Carradale	Watchful	PD269	1958
FR166	Janet	Janet	FR166			Gratitude	Gratitude	PD143	1955
FR166	St David	Janet	FR166			Green Pastures	Green Pastures	FR37	1954
FR173	Silver Fern	Gladiolus	BF255			Ha'burn	Ha'burn	BF286	1951
FR209	Branch	Silver Fern	BF369			Harvest Gleaner	Boy Peter	PD146	1955
FR136	Galilean	Gladiolus	BF255			Heather Joy 2	Summer Rose	PD341	1960
INS9	Watchful	Watchful	PD269			Hollena	Boy Peter	PD146	1955
INS310	Ha'burn	Ha'burn	BF286			Illustrious	Illustrious	PD169	1955
K616	Illustrious	Illustrious	PD169			Jeannie Stella	Jeannie Stella	RO50	1964
KY118	Heather Joy 2	Summer Rose	PD341			Lilac	Girl Doreen	PD286	1953
LH147	Shonmora	Brighter Hope	PD155			Sardonyx	Girl Doreen	PD286	1953
LH290	Summer Rose	Summer Rose	PD341			Shonmora	Brighter Hope	PD155	1956
ME188	Branch	Silver Fern	BF369			Silver Fern	Gladiolus	BF255	1951
OB39	Watchful	Watchful	PD269			Speedwell	Gratitude	PD143	1955
PD140	Boy John	Boy John	PD140			Stanhope	Girl Doreen	PD286	1953
PD143	Gratitude	Gratitude	PD143			St David	Janet	FR166	1962
PD146	Boy Peter	Boy Peter	PD146			Summer Rose	Summer Rose	PD341	1960
PD155	Brighter Hope	Brighter Hope	PD155			Vital Spark	Girl Doreen	PD286	1953
PD169	Illustrious	Illustrious	PD169			Watchful	Watchful	PD269	1958
PD269	Watchful	Watchful	PD269						
PD286	Girl Doreen	Girl Doreen	PD286						
PD341	Summer Rose	Summer Rose	PD341						
RO37	Concord	Boy Peter	PD146						
RO50	Jeannie Stella	Jeannie Stella	RO50						
SY53	Galilean	Gladiolus	BF255						
TT45	Hollena	Boy Peter	PD146						
TT93	Silver Fern	Gladiolus	BF255						
TT123	Harvest Gleaner	Boy Peter	PD146						
TT142	Heather Joy 2	Summer Rose	PD341						

Home

Tommy Summers PLN & name change reference

Yawl list

PLN	New Name	Launch Name	PLN
A372	Girl Avril	Ocean Swell	FR69
A649	Jenna Louise	Virtuous	FR353
A753	San Ray	Grateful	FR270
A753	Loyalty	Grateful	FR270
AH137	Just Reward	Just Reward	FR117
B129	Daybreak	Daybreak	FR250
B172	Graceful Morn	Sceptre	FR237
B456	Amethyst	Amethyst	FR321
BA133	Girl Avril	Ocean Swell	FR69
BA275	Be in Time	Be in Time	FR64
BA288	Lindeadar	Boy James	FR83
BCK157	Edna	Edna	BCK157
BF208	Brilliant	Brilliant	BF208
BF265	Just Reward	Just Reward	FR117
BF266	Boyne Vale	Boyne Vale	BF266
BH115	Golden Lily	Golden Lily	FR21
BRD25	Golden Lily	Golden Lily	FR21
BRD138	Morning Star	Speedwell	FR316
BRD173	Sceptre	Sceptre	FR237
BRD179	Venture	Ocean Swell	FR69
BH179	Venture	Ocean Swell	FR69
C227	Gracious	Gracious	FR167
CO830	Integrity	Boyne Vale	BF266
CT14	Harvest Moon	Harvest Moon	FR131
FD283	Boy James	Boy James	FR83
FR21	Golden Lily	Golden Lily	FR21
FH29	Fair Morn	Girl Jane	FR92
FR31	Guiding Star	Guiding Star	FR31
FR45	Winsome	Winsome	FR45
FR47	Morning Star	Morning Star	FR47
FR54	Fisher Boys	Fisher Boys	FR54
FR64	Be in Time	Be in Time	FR64
FR69	Ocean Swell	Ocean Swell	FR69
FR78	Daisy	Daisy	FR78
FR80	Golden Quest	Golden Quest	FR80
FR83	Boy James	Boy James	FR83
FR90	Lenten Rose	Lenten Rose	FR90
FR92	Girl Jane	Girl Jane	FR92
FR117	Just Reward	Just Reward	FR117
FR131	Harvest Moon	Harvest Moon	FR131
FR167	Gracious	Gracious	FR167
FR219	Girl Betty	Girl Betty	FR219
FR227	Harvest Lily	Harvest Lily	FR227
FR231	Valiant	Valiant	FR231
	Blue Max	Valiant	FR231
FR237	Sceptre	Sceptre	FR237
FR245	Shamariah	Shamariah	FR245
FR250	Daybreak	Daybreak	FR250
FR269	Accord	Edna	BCK157

PLN	New Name	Launch Name	PLN
FR270	Grateful	Grateful	FR270
FR316	Speedwell	Speedwell	FR316
FR316	Thalassa	Speedwell	FR316
FR321	Amethyst	Amethyst	FR321
FR323	Lily 2	Hopeful	PD312
FR353	Virtuous	Virtuous	FR353
FR372	Easter Morn	Easter Morn	FR372
FY43	Lenten Rose	Lenten Rose	FR90
INS9	Amethyst	Amethyst	FR321
INS40	Jenna Louise	Virtuous	FR353
INS234	Fisher Boys	Fisher Boys	FR54
K118	Hopeful	Hopeful	PD312
K210	Brilliant	Brilliant	BF208
K932	Accord	Edna	BCK157
LK1	Brilliant	Brilliant	BF208
LK213	Lowra May	Golden Quest	FR80
LK321	Osprey	Golden Quest	FR80
LK543	Girl Betty	Girl Betty	FR219
LK688	Accord	Edna	BCK157
LK987	Shamariah	Shamariah	FR245
ME34	Guiding Star	Guiding Star	FR31
ME37	Just Reward	Just Reward	FR117
OB58	Golden Lily	Golden Lily	FR21
OB275	Be in Time	Be in Time	FR64
OB372	Girl Avril	Ocean Swell	FR69
OB456	Amethyst	Amethyst	FR321
PD34	Guiding Star	Guiding Star	FR31
PD49	Jenna Louise	Virtuous	FR353
PD224	Fair Morn	Girl Jane	FR92
PD276	Just Reward	Just Reward	FR117
PD312	Hopeful	Hopeful	PD312
PD330	Virtuous	Virtuous	FR353
RY39	Daybreak	Daybreak	FR250
SA331	Harvest Moon	Harvest Moon	FR131
SY29	Daybreak	Daybreak	FR250
SY79	Lily 2	Hopeful	PD312
SY306	Brilliant	Brilliant	BF208
TN4	Redfin	Daybreak	FR250
TN4	Daybreak	Daybreak	FR250
UL20	Accord	Edna	BCK157
UL32	Harvest Lily	Harvest Lily	FR227
UL39	Fisher Boys	Fisher Boys	FR54
UL78	Jenna Louise	Virtuous	FR353
UL114	Boy Alec	Easter Morn	FR372
UL117	Golden Lily	Golden Lily	FR21
UL128	Kittiwake	Kittiwake	UL128
UL190	Hopeful	Hopeful	PD312
UL321	Saturn	Golden Quest	FR80
WK42	Lily 2	Hopeful	PD312

PLN	New Name	Launch Name	PLN
WK83	Reaper	Boy James	FR83
WK118	Brilliant	Brilliant	BF208
WK165	Accord	Edna	BCK157
WK185	Girl Betty	Girl Betty	FR219
WK420	Be in Time	Be in Time	FR64
WK455	Hopeful	Hopeful	PD312

Alphabetical order

New Name	Launch Name	PLN	Year
Accord	Edna	BCK157	1961
Blue Max	Valiant	FR231	1960
Boy Alec	Easter Morn	FR372	1953
Fair Morn	Girl Jane	FR92	1959
Girl Avril	Ocean Swell	FR69	1958
Graceful Morn	Sceptre	FR237	1956
Integrity	Boyne Vale	BF266	1962
Jenna Louise	Virtuous	FR353	1953
Lily 2	Hopeful	PD312	1959
Lindeadar	Boy James	FR83	1959
Loyalty	Grateful	FR270	1960
Lowra May	Golden Quest	FR80	1957
Morning Star	Speedwell	FR316	1962
Osprey	Golden Quest	FR80	1957
Reaper	Boy James	FR83	1959
Redfin	Daybreak	FR250	1962
San Ray	Grateful	FR270	1960
Saturn	Golden Quest	FR80	1957
Thalassa	Speedwell	FR316	1962
Venture	Ocean Swell	FR69	1958

APPENDIX B: TENDER FOR 40FT FISHING BOAT

THOMAS SUMMERS & CO.

BOAT-BUILDERS & SHIP REPAIRERS

STEAM-BOAT QUAY   ∴   NORTH BREAKWATER

FRASERBURGH

278.

15th February, 1961.

Mr. J. H. Trabes,
Langanaes,
Crofts Hill,
Flamborough.

Dear Mr. Trabes,

    We have pleasure in enclosing herewith our Tender for a
40ft. fishing boat, with all the items included we think you
require.   Should there be any alterations you wish to make,
we can go into more detail about same when you come to see us
on Monday first.

    We are preparing a full specification of the hull and
timber sizes, etc., and will have it ready for you when you call.

             Yours faithfully,
             for T. SUMMERS & CO.,

             Thomas Summers Porter

T. SUMMERS & CO., BOAT BUILDERS, FRASERBURGH

T E N D E R

To: Mr. J. H. Trabes,   14th February, 1961.
     Langanaes, Crofts Hill, Flamborough.

Dear Sir,

     In reply to your enquiry, we hereby offer to supply a motor fishing
boat as follows:-

(a)   Hull, of the following dimensions:-

             Length overall   - 40 ft. 3½
             Breadth over planking - 15 ft. 13-2
             Depth (moulded)   - 6 ft. 6 ins. ?.........£4100: -: -

(b)   (i)   Engine: Model - K3; h.p. - 66:
             Makers - Bergius Company Ltd.,
             (complete with stern gear, controls
             bilge and wash down pump, 24 volt.
             electrical starting system)
             including installation ....£1840: -: -

             1 D8C Dynamo and cut out installed. 185: -: -

       (ii) Fuel Tanks: No.2; Capacity each
             200 galls. installed .... 165: -: -   2190: -: -

(c)   (i)   Crab pot hauler installed (Maker -
             Miller, St. Monance) ....£ 140: -: -

       (ii) Electric lighting installation -
             22 points .... 235: -: -
             Kelvin Hughes MS.30 Echosounder
             installed .... 320: -: -
             Woodson RT/DF 'Clipper' model
             installed .... 240: -: -

       (iii) Sails and outfit to B.O.T.
             specification .... 295: -: -
             1 - 4" 'Whale' pump installed .....   37:10: -
             1 - 2½"'Whale' pump installed .....   22:10: -

       (iv) Fresh water tank with pump installed   57:10: -
             1 Doric Cooker installed ....   67:10: -

       (v)   2 Sets 24 volt. Batteries .... 180: -: -
             1 - 7" Card compass and binnacle
             including adjustment fee ....   30: -: -
             Cushions on seats ....   23: -: -
             Cementing vessel ....   24:10: -   1672:10: -

                     All for the sum of ....£7962:10: -

the boat to be in accordance with the specification for (a), (b) and (c)
attached and signed by us as relative hereto.

     This offer is made subject to the Terms and Conditions of Contract for
Construction of a Fishing Boat with assistance under the Sea Fish Industry
Act, 1951, and/or the White Fish and Herring Industries Act, 1953, as
adopted by the Fishing Boat Builders' Association, 14, Bon-Accord Square,
Aberdeen, and approved by the White Fish Authority on 19th August, 1953,
a copy of which is sent you herewith and which are to be held as incorporated
in and forming part of this tender.

APPENDIX C: SEA FISHING BOATS (SCOTLAND) ACT 1886 – DISCHARGE OF MORTGAGE FOR *JANET*, FR166

Sea Fishing Boats (Scotland) Act, 1886

Discharge of Mortgage A

Form No. **6.**

H.M. CUSTOMS AND EXCISE

Entered
-5 JUL 1972
1030

(1) I or We

Mortgage to secure principal sum and interest.

(1) **I** the undersigned GEORGE HERBERT TRAVES of 29 Richmond Street Bridlington in the County of Yorkshire

(2) *me or us.*

in consideration of £2601-0-0 this day lent to (2) me

by the WHITE FISH AUTHORITY of Lincolns Inn Chambers 2/3 Cursitor Street London E.C.4

do hereby bind (3) myself and (4) my heirs or executors to pay to

(3) *myself or ourselves.*
(4) *my or our.*

the said White Fish Authority

the said sum of £2601

together with interest thereon at the rate of 6½ per cent. per annum or such other rate or rates as may be fixed by the said White Fish Authority under an Agreement ~~on the .... day of .... next ; and secondly that if the said~~ dated 2nd May 1961. Secondly that ~~principal sum is not paid on the said day~~ (1) I or (4) my heirs or

executors, will, so long as the same or any part thereof remains unpaid, pay

to the said White Fish Authority interest on the whole or such

part thereof as may for the time being remain unpaid, at the ~~rate of~~ said rate

~~or rates~~ ~~per cent. per annum~~, by equal half-yearly payments on the 31st day

of March and 30th day of September in every year ; and

in security thereof (1) I hereby mortgage to the said White Fish Authority

Sixteen shares in the fishing boat named the "JANET"

of FRASERBURGH , registered No. FR166 , belonging to (2)

me ; ~~and (1) .... declare that this mortgage is made on condition that~~

~~the power of sale which by the Sea Fishing Boats (Scotland) Act, 1886, is~~

~~vested in the said .... shall not be exercised~~

~~until the said (2) .... day of ....~~. Lastly, (1) I

(5) *Insert the day fixed for payment of principal as above.*

for (3) myself and (4) my heirs and executors, hereby declare that (1) I

ha power to mortgage in manner aforesaid the above-mentioned

shares, and that the same are free from incumbrances (6).

(6) *If any prior incumbrance and "save as appears by the registry of the said boat."*

(7) *Here name and designate the two witnesses.*

In witness whereof (1) I have hereto subscribed (4) my

name this twelfth day of March , one thousand nine

hundred and sixty two in the presence of (7) P.S. Towse,

35 St. Mary's Walk Bridlington E. Yorks. P.E.M. Lewis Lloyds Bank Chambers

Quantity Surveyor Bridlington E. Yorks

Insurance Broker

P. S. Towse _____ (Witness)

G.H. Traves.

P.E.M. _____ (Witness)

Sec. F.1141 (Nov. 1954)

APPENDIX D: MODEL FORM OF BUILDING CONTRACT (INSHORE VESSELS)

WHITE FISH AUTHORITY

MODEL FORM OF
BUILDING CONTRACT (INSHORE VESSELS)

(Based on standard form of contract prepared by the Ship and Boat Builders' National Federation.)

An Agreement made the *Eleventh* day of *April*, 19 *61*, between *Thomas Summers & Co, Boatbuilders, Fraserburgh* in the County of *Aberdeen, Scotland*, England (hereinafter called "the Builders") of the one part and *Mr. G. H. Fraver, "Langanaeo", Crofts Hill, Flamborough*. (hereinafter called "the Purchaser") of the other part WHEREAS the Builders have agreed to build for the Purchaser and the Purchaser has agreed to buy the craft hereinafter described for the sum of *£ 4210 : 5 : 0 Stg.* to be paid in manner hereinafter appearing NOW IT IS HEREBY MUTUALLY AGREED between the parties hereto as follows:—

1. The Builders will lay down, construct, launch and fit out the craft to be identified by the Builders' reference number in accordance with the detailed specification and drawings annexed hereto each separate sheet bearing the signature of both parties to this Agreement.

2. The Purchaser shall pay to the Builders for the craft the sum of *£ 4210 :5/:* payment to be made as follows:—

   (a) Upon the signing hereof .. *15* % of the above sum
   (b) Upon the laying of the keel .. *5* % of the above sum
   (c) Upon completion of the planking *40* % of the above sum
   (d) Upon installation of the engine or upon stepping of the mast whichever is the earlier .. .. *30* % of the above sum
   (e) Upon completion of acceptance trials *20* % of the above sum

The Builders shall by notice in writing advise the Purchaser of the date on which instalments shall become due.

3. The Builders will use their best endeavours to complete the construction and fitting out by the *Tenth* day of *July, 1961,* but owing to the effect of delays and shortages such delivery date cannot be guaranteed.

4. In case the Builders do not proceed with reasonable despatch in the building of the vessel according to the meaning of these Presents it shall be competent for (but not incumbent upon) the Purchaser after 15 days' notice in writing to enter into the Building Yard of the Builders and to employ any number of workmen and use and employ all the machinery engines and tools of the Builders and proceed with the finishing of the vessel and for that purpose to use and employ all materials brought into the said Building Yard for the purpose of the vessel and to purchase and provide any other materials proper to be employed therein and to pay at reasonable prices for such materials and the wages of the workmen out of the balance remaining unpaid of the hereinafter mentioned instalments and in case the same shall be insufficient for the purpose then the Builders shall on demand pay and make good the deficiency other than that due to payment of overtime rates of wages.

5. Upon completion of the craft the Builders will notify the Purchaser in writing that the craft is ready for acceptance trials to be run and the Purchaser or his authorised Agent will present himself within twenty-eight days of the date of such notice to accompany the Builders or their representative upon a trial run of not less than one hour's duration but in the event of the Purchaser or his authorised Agent failing to so present himself as aforesaid then as from the expiration of the twenty-eighth day the instalment payable upon completion of the acceptance trials shall be deemed to be due and payable and the Builders shall be deemed to have fulfilled their obligations under the terms of the contract.

6. The Builders shall be deemed to have completed the construction and fitting out of the craft in accordance with the requirements of the annexed specification at the conclusion of the trial run provided that the performance of the craft during such trial run is to the reasonable satisfaction of the Purchaser such satisfaction to be indicated by the signature of the Purchaser to the memorandum endorsed on the back hereof.

7. The vessel and her propelling machinery and all materials from time to time intended for the vessel and within the Works of the Builders shall be insured by the Builders with a first class Insurance Office or at Lloyds against all Builders' Risks including war risks in accordance with "Institute Clauses for Builders' Risks amended for Yacht and Motor Boat" until delivery. In the event of the said vessel engines or equipment sustaining damage at any time before delivery any monies received in respect of the insurance shall be applied by the Builders in making good the said damage during ordinary working hours in a reasonable and workmanlike manner. The Purchasers shall not on account of the said damage or repair be entitled to reject or to make any objection to the vessel engines or equipment or to make any claim for alleged consequential loss or depreciation. At the time of delivery of the vessel to the Purchasers all liability of the Builders under this clause shall thereupon cease.

Notwithstanding the foregoing should the vessel from any cause become a total loss or deemed to be at any time a constructive arranged or compromised total loss or if the vessel engines or equipment appropriated to the contract or the Builder's yard premises plant machinery equipment or any of them should be seriously damaged by any cause whatever the Builders may in their discretion elect either to fulfil this contract or to refund to the Purchasers the instalments if any received by them and thereupon this contract will be determined in all respects as if the same had been duly completed and the Owners shall have no further right to claim on the Builders.

8. The said craft as she is constructed together with all materials equipment fittings and machinery intended for her whether in the building yard workshops water or elsewhere shall immediately become the property of the Purchaser and shall not be within the ownership or disposition of the Builders but the Builders shall at all times have a lien thereon for recovery of all sums due whether invoiced or not under the terms of this Agreement or any variation or modification thereof.

9. If any defective workmanship of the Builders and/or materials shall be discovered in the hull machinery sails or rigging (except as hereinafter provided) of the craft within six months after the acceptance trials fair wear and tear excepted and notice in writing of the same be at once given to the Builders the Builders shall either repair and make good the same or pay to the Purchaser a sum equal to the cost which they would have incurred in repairing or making good the same at their yard but the Builders shall in no case be liable for detention consequential or other damages or for any defects in either original or substituted work which shall appear after the said period of six months nor shall the Builders be liable for the failure of any proprietary articles or sub-contracted work which shall bear only the customary guarantee of the manufacturers where applicable nor shall the Builders be responsible for any fault or failure consequent upon the design of the craft should such design not be the work of the Builders or any Naval Architect appointed by them upon their own responsibility. Every guarantee and/or warranty and/or condition implied by Statute or common law is expressly excluded from this contract.

10. The Purchaser or his authorised Agent shall have free access to the craft and to the materials to be used in the construction of the craft for the purpose of inspection at any time during the normal business hours of the Builders' establishment. Any such person using any part of the Builders' premises does so at his own risk. The White Fish Authority, or their agents, shall also have the right to enter, at their own risk, the Builders' yard, workshops and the vessel for the purpose of inspecting materials and workmanship at any time during ordinary working hours, but the Builders shall not be obliged to take instructions from them.

11. Any modifications to the annexed specification shall be incorporated in a supplementary agreement in writing made between and signed by the parties hereto.

12. In the event of any instalment remaining unpaid for twenty-eight days after becoming due the Builders shall be entitled to interest at the rate of five per cent per annum and after a further period of twenty-eight days shall be at liberty to sell the craft as she may then lie or may complete and sell the craft after completion and any loss on such re-sale shall be made good by the Purchaser.

13. All drawings specifications and plans prepared by the Builders or their Architects shall remain the property of the Builders in so far as any copyright therein is reserved to them.

14. In the event of any rise or fall in the cost of labour and/or materials between the date of the signing hereof and the completion of this contract the Builders shall increase or decrease the total sum specified in Clause 2 hereof, in accordance with the actual variation in the costs of construction of the vessel or machinery under these headings, duly certified by the Builders' Auditors.

15. Delivery will be given at the Builders' premises or on the water adjacent thereto.

16. If any dispute difference or question arise between the Parties hereto during or after the construction of the craft relating to the rights duties or obligations of either party hereunder the same shall be referred to the arbitration of a single arbitrator to be agreed upon by the parties hereto and this Agreement shall be deemed to be a submission to arbitration within the Arbitration Acts, 1889 to 1934 or any Statutory provisions for the time being in force.

17. This Agreement is to be construed and take effect as a Contract made in England/Scotland and in accordance with the Laws of England/Scotland and the Purchasers hereby submit to the jurisdiction of the High Court of Justice in England/Scotland. All notices to the Builders concerning this contract shall be addressed to the Builders at

All notices to the Purchasers concerning this contract shall be addressed to the Purchasers at

For THOMAS SUMMERS & CO.

Thomas Summers

SIGNED BY THE BUILDERS...
IN THE PRESENCE OF
    Witness ....
    Address ....
    ....

    Occupation..
SIGNED BY THE PURCHASER......*C. H. Travis*
IN THE PRESENCE OF
    Witness ......*L. J. Atkinson*
    Address ......Monument Garage
    ......Flamborough.
    Occupation......Motor Engineer

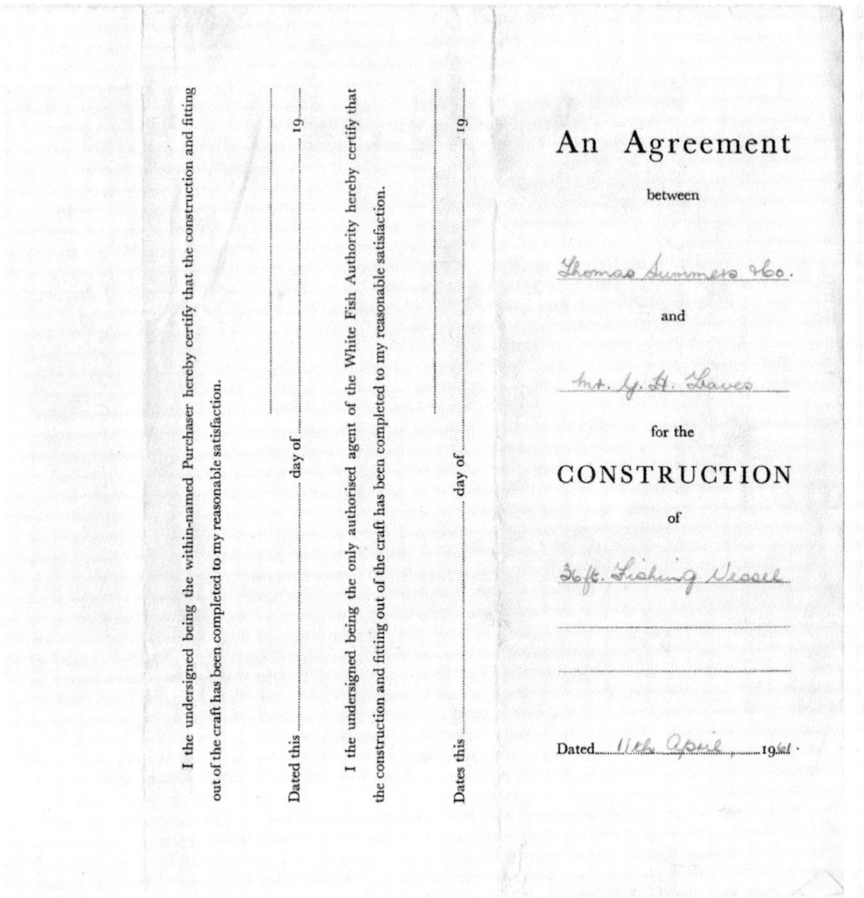

An Agreement

between

Thomas Summers &Co.

and

Mr. G. H. Lawes

for the

CONSTRUCTION

of

36ft. Fishing Vessel

Dated 11th April 19 61.

I the undersigned being the within-named Purchaser hereby certify that the construction and fitting out of the craft has been completed to my reasonable satisfaction.

Dated this _____ day of _____ 19____

I the undersigned being the only authorised agent of the White Fish Authority hereby certify that the construction and fitting out of the craft has been completed to my reasonable satisfaction.

Dates this _____ day of _____ 19____

APPENDIX E: PLANS OF A YAWL BY MALCOLM BURGE (MB DRAFTING)

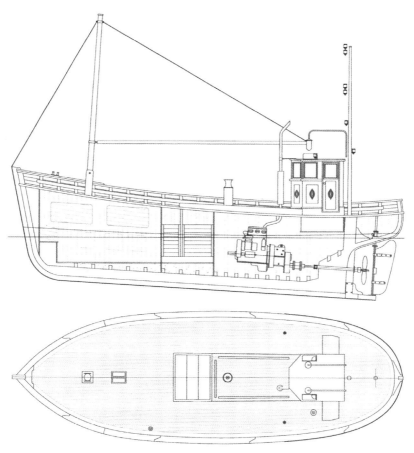

T Summers & Co 33ft Fraserburgh Yawl
42hp 3LW Gardner engine
Malcolm Burge © COPYRIGHT 2019

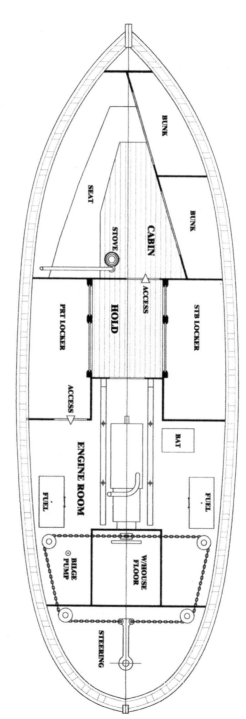

T Summers & Co 33ft Fraserburgh Yawl
Internal Plan
Malcolm Burge © COPYRIGHT 2019

APPENDIX F: ADVERT FOR THOMAS SUMMERS & CO.

SOUNDLY CONSTRUCTED FISHING BOATS

The Craft illustrated shows a recent construction on acceptance trials.

★ Length O.A. 73 ft. Breadth 20 ft. Draught 9 ft. 6 in. Powered by 152 h.p. Gardner Diesel Engine providing a speed of 9 knots. Fitted with 4 speed seine net winch and Beccles coiler. Radio Transmitter, direction finder and Kelvin-Hughes Echo Sounder. This traditional ship can carry a catch of 300 crans of herring in fish room.

THOMAS SUMMERS & CO.

STEAM-BOAT QUAY · NORTH BREAKWATER
FRASERBURGH

APPENDIX G: DRAWING OF
A FRASERBURGH RIPPER LINE

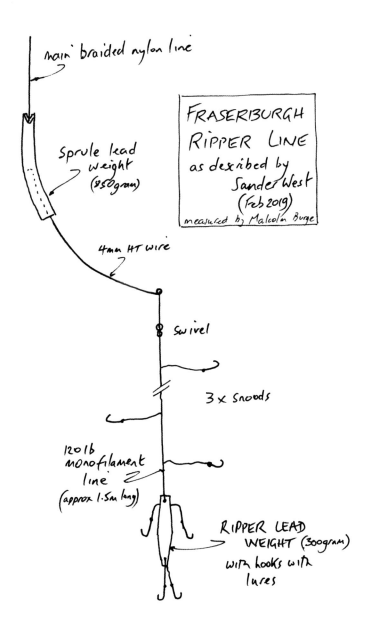

main braided nylon line

Sprule lead
weight
(850gram)

FRASERBURGH
RIPPER LINE
as described by
Sander West
(Feb 2019)
measured by Malcolm Burge

4mm HT wire

swivel

3 x snoods

120lb
monofilament
line
(approx 1.5m long)

RIPPER LEAD
WEIGHT (300gram)
with hooks with
lures

BIBLIOGRAPHY

Cranna, John, *Fraserburgh: Past and Present* (The Rosemount Press, 1914)

MacDonald, Bill, *Boats & Builders: The History of Boatbuilding Around Fraserburgh* (MacDonald & Co., 1993)

MacDonald, Bill, *Fraserburgh Harbour: The Boom Years* (Y. MacDonald, 1995)

Smylie, Mike, *The Tweed to the Northern Isles: The Fishing Industry Through Time* (Amberley Publishing, 2013)

Wilson, Gloria, *Scottish Fishing Craft* (Fishing News, 1965)

Wilson, Gloria, *More Scottish Fishing Craft* (Fishing News, 1968)

MORE FROM
THE HISTORY PRESS

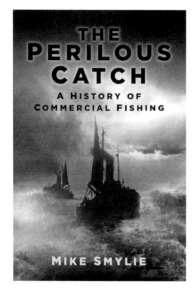